Glazed America

UNIVERSITY PRESS OF FLORIDA

Florida A&M University, Tallahassee
Florida Atlantic University, Boca Raton
Florida Gulf Coast University, Ft. Myers
Florida International University, Miami
Florida State University, Tallahassee
New College of Florida, Sarasota
University of Central Florida, Orlando
University of Florida, Gainesville
University of North Florida, Jacksonville
University of South Florida, Tampa
University of West Florida, Pensacola

UNIVERSITY PRESS OF FLORIDA

GAINESVILLE · TALLAHASSEE · TAMPA · BOCA RATON · PENSACOLA · ORLANDO · MIAMI · JACKSONVILLE · FT. MYERS · SARASOTA

America

A History of the Doughnut

PAUL R. MULLINS

13 12 11 10 09 08   6 5 4 3 2 1

Library of Congress Cataloging-in-Publication Data
Mullins, Paul R., 1962–
Glazed America : a history of the doughnut / Paul R. Mullins.
p. cm.
Includes bibliographical references and index.
ISBN 978-0-8130-3238-2 (alk. paper)
1. Doughnuts. 2. Food habits—United States. I. Title.
TX770.D67M85 2008
641.8'653—dc22   2008002544

The University Press of Florida is the scholarly publishing agency
for the State University System of Florida, comprising Florida A&M
University, Florida Atlantic University, Florida Gulf Coast University,
Florida International University, Florida State University, New College
of Florida, University of Central Florida, University of Florida, University of North Florida, University of South Florida, and University of
West Florida.

University Press of Florida
15 Northwest 15th Street
Gainesville, FL 32611–2079
http://www.upf.com

Contents

Acknowledgments

When John Byram wondered if I could envision a book on doughnuts, I was surprised that I had such strong feelings about fried dough, and I instantly visited the local doughnut shop. Aided by a few delightfully sweet Long's Bakery doughnuts, John convinced me that there was a book in the subject and helped shepherd the volume through publication. He should receive the credit for recognizing an interesting topic, helping me frame the subject, and serving as a firm and fair sounding board. Mark Warner convinced me that a food history would be interesting and challenging. Aaron Method assembled the documentation, took care of a range of unpleasant research tasks, and wondered what the book was really about. Wade Tharp took a bunch of excellent pictures of local doughnut shops at the last minute. Dennis Rinehart of Long's Bakery was nice enough to share the history of the bakery, allow us to take some pictures, and share some of his family's pictures of the bakery. My colleagues at Indiana University–Purdue University, Indianapolis were curious about the subject and needled me on it on a regular basis. Thanks to Larry Zimmerman, Peg Williams, Liz Kryder-Reid, Rick Ward, Chris Glidden, Sue Hyatt, Jeanette Dickerson-Putman, Melissa Bingmann, and Owen Dwyer for discussing various pieces of the project. Owen Dwyer told me about bearbaiting and connected me with Matthew McCourt, who framed most of what I ended up thinking about bears and doughnuts. Andy Roberts talked to me about life at Long's Bakery in the late 1950s. Cat Daddy at VooDoo Doughnuts took some pictures of his shop for me and electronically discussed the state of doughnuts. Jen Graham at the University Press of Florida was exceptionally helpful assembling images and getting the book in order.

My son, Aidan, was happy to find out that we would be required to eat some doughnuts as a research task, even though we didn't really eat enough to satisfy him. My wife, Marlys, understands the craft of writing far better than I do and was completely supportive. She helped me finish this book while quietly writing and finishing several of her own.

of these folks hail from the city's northern and far-western suburbs, others walk to the shop from nearby neighborhoods, and others arrive in cars from neighborhoods throughout the westside. It is difficult to stereotype the consumers' ethnicity. Some are white, their ethnic origins ranging from the British Isles to almost any point in Europe, and others are African Americans, most descended from southerners who came in various midwestern migrations between Reconstruction and World War II. Since Long's has no "sit-and-sip" space, this rather complicated demographic streams out the door holding white boxes destined for kitchen tables, front seats, workplaces, and offices.

The broad social patterns that fuel doughnut consumption vary from one place to the next, yet doughnuts' allure tends to cross social lines. When Long's first turned on its sign, the surrounding community included a range of working-class people, some marginalized by economic scarcity and others by racism and cultural xenophobia. The Haughville community south of Long's emerged in the nineteenth century alongside factories and railroad yards that provided steady if unpleasant and modest-paying labor to what was at first a European immigrant community. By World War II a mix of African Americans and Appalachian whites had made their homes in Haughville, and many of their descendants continue to call the community home today. To the west, modest suburbs instantly sprung up around the Speedway and Westside businesses in the early twentieth century. Most of these neighborhoods practiced various forms of white exclusivity that created a lingering racially based mosaic throughout the city's Westside. By the 1980s and 1990s, suburban communities rapidly sprang up even further to the west as Indianapolis mushroomed outward like most American cities.

Like most of the fast-food restaurants that emerged in America during the cold war, Long's has historically catered to a highly mobile community that commuted along one of the thoroughfares leading into the city from outlying communities. Long's opened two years after the last streetcar was retired in Indianapolis, and when its ovens first came on most residents were already car commuters who entered the city along routes like West Sixteenth. In the 1960s a popular drive-in sat directly alongside Long's serving burgers and fast food to local teens, and a restaurant sat across the street in a building that eventually became a strip club. However, an interstate circling the city was on the horizon,

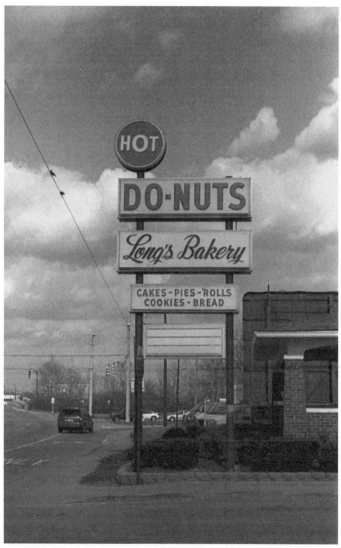

Since 1955, the prominent "Hot Do-nuts" sign over Long's Bakery has celebrated the Indianapolis bakery's most popular item. (Photograph courtesy of Wade Terrell Tharp.)

and many commuters would soon move into fresh suburbs far removed from Long's. The surrounding neighborhood changed significantly when suburban flight and urban renewal bled the city from the 1950s onward. Much of the community around Long's became dominated by families living in modest and once-solid homes that were beginning to show their age. Many of the factories closest to these neighborhoods also moved into suburbs or simply closed altogether.

Long's has witnessed and even flourished in the face of a relatively typical tale of spatial transformation, demographic shifts, and quite radical changes in how Americans have eaten in the last century. Little shops like Long's are prominent social spaces in many communities, and doughnuts made by modest bakeries and global chains alike are celebrated by many consumers. Yet the transformations wrought by car culture and mass foodways have not been universally applauded, and doughnuts often have been scapegoats for public health transformations that are considered symptomatic of widespread inability to control our own desires. That internally dissentious story is similar to the complex social and historical insights that emerge from most foodways analysis. Food histories spin exceptionally complicated social tales about the rich relationships between people across time, space, ethnic lines, and national boundaries. Each morning, for instance, the lowly doughnut bonds consumers and producers in fleeting relationships across time and space, much as it has over two centuries. For the most part, though, our attention is focused on eating doughnuts and does not typically contemplate doughnuts' social symbolism or the complicated agricultural, marketing, and production system that delivers doughnuts to us.

Eating a doughnut is in itself not all that interesting, even though for many of us it is a superbly pleasurable moment. What is more interesting is what doughnut consumption and doughnut shops symbolize, the broader social patterns that shape doughnut consumption, and what foods like doughnuts can tell us about the social and historical settings in which they are consumed. At one level, the doughnut story is partly about the history of fried pastries, but it is also a history of retail strips like Sixteenth Street, the social transformations in how we have eaten in the twentieth century, and a cultural insight into the people who frequent shops like Long's. This history of doughnuts reveals the most

Generations of travelers passed along Route 66 between Chicago and California making stops at restaurants like the Donut Drive-In in St. Louis, which opened in 1951. Such restaurants beckoned hungry travelers with prominent marquees, convenient roadside access, and easy parking. (Photograph courtesy of Bygonebyways.com.)

significant contours of twentieth-century food consumption, yet at another level the doughnut provides an insight into the meanings we invest in highly disputed public "doughnut discourses." Like any piece of material culture whose meaning is publicly contested, doughnuts provide an insight into who we want to be and who we think we are, so they do not simply reflect the objective facts of our social and cultural identities or historical context. For one person a doughnut may be an everyday food that is eaten without much thought; for another it may represent the hazard of descent into obesity; and for another it may well be a symbol of nationalism, class, and many more dimensions of consumer identity.

Doughnuts embody complex social and historical connections in American life, and our disagreements over the doughnut's meaning reflect the ways in which various people hope to shape American society. Consequently, some of this story involves relatively straightforward historical examination of fried dough over several centuries. Yet much of this book revolves around how everyday doughnut discussions provide a way to negotiate critical dimensions of consumer identity, such as class, body image, or nationalism. That is, how have we talked about ourselves in public discussions of doughnuts? Can we learn much of anything about American society over the past century or two by examining how we have publicly discussed doughnuts? What would a history of twentieth-century America look like if written from the perspective of the many people who make and consume fried dough?

The first chapter takes a look at the basic ideas that frame the doughnut. Any meaningful piece of material culture has conflicted meanings, and doughnuts certainly reveal deeply divided feelings about a range of things. Commodities like doughnuts reveal complicated connections, yet doughnuts also are symbolic battlegrounds over the tangled depths of personal and collective identity. Doughnuts can be delightful comfort foods eaten in significant community spaces, but they also are part of the landscape on which we discuss things like what it means to be American or working class or to have proper body discipline.

The second chapter traces the historical contours of doughnut production and consumption since antiquity and examines how that history has shaped doughnuts' social symbolism. Fried dough has its origins in the distant reaches of the Neolithic Revolution, but doughnuts as we know them are a much more recent arrival. Doughnuts emerged from a Dutch dish known as olykoek in the eighteenth century, and over the course of the subsequent century they became a relatively commonplace American food. Doughnuts rapidly became an American dish, and by the mid-nineteenth century they assumed the spherical shape that we now associate with a doughnut. In the twentieth century the doughnut became part of national cuisine with the advent of mass-produced doughnuts sold in chain marketing outlets. The doughnut's ascent over the twentieth century reflects how American cities changed as the car, mass production, suburbanization, and consumer prosperity transformed American foodways.

The third chapter probes the complicated relationship between doughnut marketing and demand. The rather prosaic doughnut is routinely associated with nationalist fervor, class distinctions, and a variety of significant sentiments that frame how we see ourselves and society, though we could also say this of beer, chips, and many more foods. Marketers attempt to marshal this symbolism, and some doughnut manufacturers' appeals to discourses like nationalism have been quite successful. However, appealing dimensions of doughnut consumption like the literal and social atmosphere of a doughnut shop are complicated influences on how doughnuts are made, sold, and eaten. Consequently, understanding doughnut desire and demand requires us to look at the context of consumption beyond the moment a cruller goes into our stomach.

The fourth chapter looks at how doughnuts have been "moralized" as mechanisms with which we contest deep-seated dimensions of American life. On the one hand, many commentators are concerned about doughnuts' negative effect on consumers, especially their physical impacts but also extending into more ambiguous moral and disciplinary effects. On the other hand, a range of doughnut defenders are worried that the significant consumer rights invested in doughnut consumption are now under fire and at risk. Doughnuts occupy a contentious landscape in which many foods are simply cast as "good" or "bad," and much of this doughnut discussion revolves around issues of health. These discussions move beyond simply questioning the fat content of a doughnut, though; instead, they illustrate that issues like community health and consumer taxation are truly public, state concerns impressed into doughnuts' meanings. This makes doughnuts' consumption a complicated act of both empowerment and disempowerment with contextually specific meanings for various consumers.

Some dimensions of doughnuts' meaning are indeed completely prosaic, and in other ways those meanings reflect much deeper and more significant public symbolism and discord. We may feel a little reluctant to grant doughnuts the status of scholarly research subjects, but few classes of material culture are more meaningful than food. Regardless of the caricatures attached to a food like doughnuts, they reflect many of the most important historical and social patterns in twentieth-century America, if not the world, so it makes some sense to confront both those stereotypes and that history. Ultimately, doughnuts deserve systematic and reflective thinking as much as most classic scholarly subjects, even as we remain critical of their significance and wary of the limits to which we can interpret the twentieth century based simply on the heritage of making and eating fried dough. Such an analysis should illuminate how we have talked about our society by discussing doughnuts and how consumption of doughnuts reveals both dominant social sentiments and internal discord over such sentiments. Doughnuts are social in the sense that they create relationships between people and illuminate commonalities and differences between various groups. Rather than assessing doughnuts in isolation from broader social and historical context, we will examine how their marketing and consumption reveal complex relationships and patterns that tell us a lot about ourselves.

1

"The Church of Krispy Kreme"

After a visit to New York City's first Krispy Kreme, Nora Ephron declared that "the sight of all those doughnuts marching solemnly to their fate makes me proud to be an American." Ephron was captivated by the Krispy Kreme shop, which cleverly celebrated retro styling, showcased an ingenious "doughnut machine," and saturated the air with the distinctive smell of sugar, yeast, and flour. Indeed, Ephron argued that the store had "become a shrine, complete with pilgrims, fanatics, converts, and proselytizers—the sort of religious experience New Yorkers like me are far more receptive to than the ones that actually involve God."[1]

It may seem absurd that an apparently innocuous doughnut could be wrapped in the flag and lent an air of religiosity, but few dimensions of our world say as much about us as food. The things we eat illuminate a complex knot of nationalism, culture, class, regionalism, economic systems, and even morality and politics. Weatherman Willard Scott echoed Ephron's passion for doughnuts and elevated doughnuts to articles of faith when he pronounced that "I belong to the church of Krispy Kreme."[2] Even the more laconic southern transplant Roy Blount gushed that "when Krispy Kremes are hot, they are to other doughnuts what angels are to people."[3]

People have remarkably strong sentiments about doughnuts, but many of us find it hard to elevate krullers to the status of mirrors for American society. We seem to harbor both fondness and embarrassment for doughnuts, and that ambivalence has complex roots. For many observers, doughnuts are symbols of temptation, unhealthiness, and personal weakness. One 2003 assessment of the most unhealthy American foods placed chocolate doughnuts near the top of the list,

Even world-class athletes are susceptible to the desire for a doughnut, as reflected in Lance Armstrong's 2003 consumption of a Krispy Kreme doughnut at a charity ride rest stop. (Photograph © Bob Daemmrich/CORBIS.)

proclaiming that "although 'bad doughnuts' may seem redundant, the chocolate-covered varieties cross the line into evil."[4] Doughnuts are routinely transformed into such transparent moral symbols, and for some observers the doughnut symbolizes the widespread self-deception Americans weave around foodways and health. *Salon*'s Mary MacVean seemed shocked to find that ostensibly health-conscious California quietly boasted 2,632 doughnut shops by her count, easily twice more than any other state, and Los Angeles's 1,650 shops makes for one of the planet's highest per capita doughnut-shop densities.[5]

It seems obvious that a steady diet of bear claws would have significant public health consequences, and the health impact of American foodways is definitely worth tackling as a pressing public concern.

Nevertheless, we will be hard-pressed to understand any food consumption—and potentially change those patterns—if food is simply boiled down to its caloric count and nutritional content and draped in transparent moralizing. We eat emotionally and in socially distinct ways, so very few foodways are utterly rational results of critical reflection on some dominant definition of "good" nutrition or "appropriate" foods. We tend to be attached to particular marketers and consumer spaces, and our consumption is directly linked to historical context, class standing, regionalism, and cultural breeding, among other things. Consequently, it is essential to understand these complicated social dimensions of food if we hope to truly fathom its complexities.

The Doughnut Battlefield

What distinguishes doughnuts from most other foods is the distinctive battlefield framed by doughnut consumption. The likes of Nora Ephron and Roy Blount elevate doughnuts to spiritual items, and streams of consumers line up each day at doughnut shops throughout the world or circle around doughnut boxes at their workplaces. Singer Carnie Wilson underwent gastric bypass surgery to control her weight gain, yet she remains so enamored with doughnuts that they arouse her: "I have hallucinations with doughnuts all the time. I'm obsessed. I get horny when I eat doughnuts."[6] Yet many observers see such an eroticized embrace of foods like doughnuts as a critical symptom of social and even moral decline that reflects our self-absorption, an erosion in personal discipline, and the spiraling expansion of the marketplace into everyday life. Even a remorseful Cookie Monster has felt compelled to counsel children that doughnuts are at best a "sometimes food."[7] In an effort to explain its conflicted popularity, a Los Angeles doughnut consumer conceded that "the doughnut is a food of shame."[8] An Oregon customer agreed, suggesting that "there's nothing more synonymous with obesity and an unhealthy lifestyle than doughnuts."[9]

Those pronouncements, oddly enough, came from people who were themselves eating doughnuts, which indicates the internal dissension some doughnut consumers feel. Doughnuts have been the target of especially virulent public vilification from a host of observers, but doughnut consumption still has generally steamed along quite profitably for the last half century. Observers hoping to reduce the consumption of foods like doughnuts have devoted much of their energy to trumpeting the nutritional downsides of doughnuts, but this ignores that much of the attraction of doughnuts—and most foods—lies beyond pure dietary considerations. Few people likely eat doughnuts because they consider them "healthy." In the face of "low-carb" diets and a host of other challenges to doughnuts, some observers—and even a few doughnut makers—divined the doughnuts' imminent demise. Despite such discordant sentiments over doughnuts, though, at the 2003 height of the low-carb movement the doughnut business grew at a rate more than double the national restaurant industry average.[10]

Food is often considered the last holdout from encroaching mass culture, a broad set of social practices defined by marketers and cultural elite that risks replacing all the truly meaningful cultural dimensions of our lives. The reasoning is that we may succumb to shopping at the mall and stocking our homes with mass-produced baubles, but we tend to stubbornly cling to foods that are much like those of our ancestors, friends, and family. Consequently, the onslaught of Coca-Cola and Starbucks is sometimes considered a critical dilution of cultural distinction, and the arrival of McDonald's is often greeted with more hostility than a new government. Doughnuts occupy a rather distinctive position along the continuum ranging from foods as emblems of cultural and household identity to foods as symbols of mass food production. Some families do make their own doughnuts and include their consumption in important seasonal or social activities, and in many instances they have done so for generations. Mormon elder Russell M. Nelson even linked doughnut consumption to traditional gender roles when he told a church General Conference that "Tonight I am attending with a son, sons-in-law, and grandsons. Where are their mothers? Gathered in the kitchen of our home! What are they doing? Making large batches of homemade doughnuts! And when we return home, we will feast on those doughnuts. . . . It's a nice family tradition, symbolic of the fact that everything we learn and do as priesthood bearers should bless our families."[11]

Nevertheless, doughnuts are a mass-produced food most closely associated with professional bakers and chain marketers like Dunkin'

Donuts, Tim Hortons, and Krispy Kreme, and because making doughnuts is a messy and somewhat demanding process, relatively few of us
produce our own. In contrast, we can always sidestep the likes of Mc-
Donald's and Starbucks and make a hamburger or a latte at home. If we
want to celebrate doughnuts as emblems of ethnic identity in the way
ham hocks are often (somewhat mechanically) associated with African
American culture, doughnuts do not emerge from a comparably rich
ethnic heritage. Perhaps the Dutch can make some primordial claim to
parenting doughnuts as we know them today, but the consumption of
doughnuts crosses all sorts of ethnic boundaries over roughly two centuries. Instead, doughnuts' meanings are significantly shaped by the
doughnut-shop experience and twentieth-century mass production, so
doughnuts loom as commodities firmly ensconced in mass consumer
space.

The caricature of doughnuts as meaningless commodities without
social or cultural consequence is clearly dealt a blow by the strong feelings doughnuts evoke. An excited Californian awaiting the opening of
a Krispy Kreme said that the doughnuts "took me back to my childhood, a time when a cream-filled doughnut could make everything better."[12] That certainly seems a great burden to be borne by doughnuts,
but for many people doughnuts evoke fond memories of family breakfasts, community gatherings, and local independent and chain bakeries
alike. Many churches, for instance, have long featured doughnuts in
communal gatherings, and many schools hold "Doughnuts with Dad"
programs at which fathers and their children bond over bakery confections. A parent-teacher organization official in California lamented
that their daytime gatherings typically drew only a dozen guests, but
she was pleasantly surprised to find that seventy-five fathers and two
hundred children showed up for a doughnut breakfast.[13]

Like many other foods, doughnuts can be the glue binding communities. One Boston retiree considered his local doughnut shop a community networking space: "You need your car fixed, there's a mechanic.
You need your pipes fixed, there's a plumber."[14] After September 2004
hurricanes in Florida, President Bush joined hurricane relief teams
handing out supplies. Their aid package included the rather odd combination of water, ice, cereal, beef jerky, mustard, and Dunkin' Donuts.
One group of Baptists in New York City more effectively spread the

word by distributing nine hundred Krispy Kremes to potential converts.[15]

Such a symbolically charged food would seem ideally suited to reflective scholarly analysis. Scholars, though, have tended to celebrate foods
that seem to have concrete roots in distinctive cultural traditions, and
less attention has been devoted to mass-produced indulgences like
doughnuts. Despite the significant amount of public discussion on
doughnuts, contemplation of doughnuts routinely descends into snick-
ers and stock caricatures. Doughnuts typically are reduced to cops' dietary cornerstone and the fare of working-class stiffs personified by
the likes of Homer Simpson. In other minds, they loom as powerful
symbols of Americans' collective descent into obesity. Diet manuals
often consider doughnuts among dieters' most challenging obstacles,
and many dieticians and public health advocates conclude that doughnuts simply "have nothing to offer."[16] One enterprising Chicago entrepreneur recognized the enormous allure of doughnuts and marketed
a delicious and very profitable low-fat doughnut. Unfortunately, his
doughnuts actually had been purchased at a neighborhood bakery and
packaged in a box claiming they had three grams of fat, which was fifteen grams less than they actually harbored.[17] Much of the discussion
of doughnuts simply casts them as "unhealthy" without wrestling with
how and why "healthiness" is defined in particular ways. Surprisingly,
few thinkers have examined why doughnuts are so popular in the first
place. The emotional appeal and social role of doughnuts and bakeries
seem to pass unexamined as we incredulously count calories yet again.
This risks ignoring how Americans have been socialized to associate
pleasure with fatty foods like doughnuts. The potential appearance of
celebrating an indulgent if not "dangerous" food has rendered doughnuts the subject of little rigorous or critical analysis.

Popular discussion about doughnuts may be a mirror of our society,
but it is a complex and often distorted image. In many ways this is the
case for all popular culture, which tends to exaggerate the extraordi-
nary dimensions of our otherwise ordinary lives. Many of us wrestle
with desire as Homer Simpson does, but few flesh-and-blood mortals
can embrace all the bodily desires Homer embraces. Since many of us
have genuine misgivings about body image, it is not surprising that
popular discourses address these apparent dilemmas by pillorying a

few foods that seem to be leading the assault on our waistlines. The attack on doughnuts, though, often overinflates their actual capacity to kill or isolates doughnut consumption from other unhealthy foodways. Much of the attack on doughnuts also at least unintentionally vilifies the things many people most cherish about doughnuts, such as their local doughnut shop's place in the community and the meaningful relationships people forge over doughnuts. The result is a public discussion that caricatures doughnuts' genuine social meanings and evades the underlying things that make doughnuts so meaningful in the first place.

Food often has such disputed symbolism because it is at the heart of our identities and significantly influences how we see ourselves individually and collectively. Most people likely occupy an ambivalent middle ground where doughnuts are delightful indulgences that uncomfortably illuminate our shortcomings in personal discipline. When we talk about doughnuts, that discussion reveals our politics, class, and culture and illuminates complicated underlying sentiments toward consumer culture, global capitalism, and body discipline. This may seem a lot to project onto a doughnut, but in fact many foods have similarly powerful social and cultural significance. Americans have long had very strong feelings about food, and in many ways the dissension over doughnuts is part of a long historical tradition that has witnessed battles over foods ranging from fried chicken to TV dinners to lattes. Doughnuts stand in a distinctive pantheon of contemporary foods that are simultaneously reviled as they are consumed in prodigious quantities: Krispy Kremes share company with Big Macs, Coca-Cola, mocha frappucinos, and comparable foods that are targets for harrowing critique even as they enjoy widespread consumption and zealous defenders.

Clearly, doughnut consumption provides some surprisingly consequential insights into American life. If we want to understand doughnuts—or for that matter any foodways or material culture—we need to understand the context in which doughnuts have been made and consumed. From the outset we need to acknowledge that doughnuts have the potential to reveal a great deal about culture, class, regionalism, and marketing and consumption if we can dismantle and push beyond superficial observations or our own deep-seated preconceptions. Doughnut consumption reflects the dynamic meanings assumed by

In 2002 Krispy Kreme announced its expansion into New England, staking a claim in the heart of Dunkin' Donuts territory. In December a mobile Krispy Kreme temporarily provided doughnuts at this future location in Medford, Massachusetts. (Photograph courtesy of tacquitos.net.)

commodities, the profound consequence of food, the social symbolism projected onto marketers, and the moralizing that a host of observers associate with particular consumption patterns. Wrapping all these subjects within doughnuts provides a surprisingly compelling insight into foodways, American identity, and modern consumer culture.

The Almighty Doughnut

In June 2004 the leaders of the world's eight most powerful industrial nations met in Sea Island, Georgia, for the Group of Eight Summit. Leaders of Canada, France, Germany, Italy, Japan, Russia, the United Kingdom, and the host United States gathered to consider, among other weighty issues, global HIV vaccine development, a polio eradication initiative, and shared military operations. Eighty-five miles south of the well-defended island, the world press corps and an army of diplomats and demonstrators sat in Savannah monitoring the summit. Eager to make a good impression on these supporting players, the U.S. delegation arranged to have a Krispy Kreme trailer trucked to Savan-

Glazed America

nah. Savannah diners can choose from a host of restaurants featuring a distinctive southern low-country cuisine borrowing from African American, Native American, and European foodways. Nevertheless, the feature attraction for much of the G8 press corps and foreign delegates was Krispy Kreme, which produced twelve hundred doughnuts an hour from a mobile bakery that the *Washington Post* snidely referred to as a "mobile biological weapons lab."[18]

Featuring Krispy Kremes before the eyes of the world suggests they are more than Homer Simpson's dietary staple. Still, it is hard for many of us to comprehend that the nation's cuisine—if not its very culture—might be appropriately represented by a doughnut. Doughnuts' capacity to evoke national pride may seem undermined by the contrasting effort to reduce them to "biological weapons," but this really illuminates the powerful and often conflicting feelings many of us have over food. If the G8 had dined the world with Coca-Cola, granola, caviar, Shake 'n Bake, or any other food, it could never have accommodated everybody's feelings about the symbolism associated with foods. The discord in this case had less to do with doughnuts than with the ambiguous notion of "American culture." Being "American" blankets a host of deep-seated class divisions, ethnic distinctions, regional identities, and conflicts over national identity, and in various minds doughnut cuisine may represent either our proudest collective moment or a national embarrassment.

Anthropologists have always understood that eating is among the most social acts people have shared across time. The moment our earliest hominid relatives gathered at central base camps and began to share food production and consumption was a critical juncture that did not simply ensure our literal survival; the acquisition, distribution, and consumption of food established a social framework within which labor roles, kin relations, and even group identity began to coalesce. No sophisticated understanding of humans' material needs and desires could preclude some consideration of eating, and a reasonably complex vision of foodways must confront endless socially and historically distinct cycles of production, distribution, desire, and satiation.

Nevertheless, some observers have tended to simplify foodways and ignore or evade their social complexity. Some scholars, for example, look at food primarily in terms of how it reflects humans' endless battle

against nature and the environment; that is, peoples' lives are funda-
mentally structured if not determined by the everyday battle to secure
sufficient food that will maximize our health and lifespans. This may
have some modest explanatory power in the most marginal environmental conditions or the distant reaches of prehistory, but even then
it simply reduces eating to caloric intake and strips food consumption
of all social context and desire. Scholars interested in the emergence
and growth of material consumption in the past half millennium have
given a lot of attention to mass commodities and shifts in marketing,
but food has often been oddly missing from such scholarship. Still more
observers seem to sidestep foodways because they are not "rational."
For example, a straightforward economic analysis of foodways would
suggest that our choices of foods and eating venues will be largely determined by economic constraints and environmental circumstance;
foodways, though, are notoriously complicated practices that reach
beyond calories, cost, and even culture, resulting in many "irrational"
consumption patterns.

As anthropologists and historians have surveyed the range of foodways folks have embraced over millennia, what becomes clear is that
what people consider "good" and "bad" is overwhelmingly social. As
Sidney Mintz puts it, "We appear to be capable of eating (and liking)
just about anything that is not immediately toxic."[19] Caloric intake in
itself is not especially interesting, and the cost of foods actually ends
up saying surprisingly little about consumption. What is much more
telling is how we decide on appropriate foods, the way socioeconomic
systems produce and deliver those foods to consumers, and how food
and eating is perhaps the most critical dimension of everyday life. Indeed, the social, marketing, and personal relationships surrounding
food matter as much as how food literally sustains us.

Since we have such strong feelings about food, we often disagree
about what it really means, and disputes over food's symbolism often
revolve around weighty social issues like identity, power, and culture.
All of the material world is equally open to dispute, and commodities
routinely loom as points for social conflict. Barbies, for instance, are
celebrated by some consumers as models that "girls can be anything"
even as other observers deride the doll as a negative image of feminin-

ity. Despite such radically different meanings ascribed to the same objects, material things are not "blank slates": a Barbie or a Krispy Kreme cannot symbolize absolutely anything. Nonetheless, most material culture is sufficiently symbolically ambiguous that its meaning is open to a reasonable range of interpretations that can buttress competing views of the world.

Disagreement over doughnuts' meaning often illuminates many of our competing visions of the world. For instance, the Mohegan Sun Casino was created by the Mohegan Tribe of Connecticut in 1996. The Mohegan have lived in the region for ten millennia. Long after James Fenimore Cooper pronounced the demise of the last of the "Mohicans" in 1826, the Mohegan became a sovereign federally recognized Indian nation in 1994. The tribal casino built shortly afterward is a stunning space that showcases Mohegan aesthetics that aspire to "transport visitors to the ancestral world of the Mohegan tribe."[20] The casino celebrates a culture that has no tangible historical link to doughnuts, but at the heart of the casino sit three Krispy Kreme shops blasting a sugary flour smell across the craps tables. The Mohegans' traditional Creation Story quilt may seem somewhat incongruous with the retro colors of the nearby Krispy Kreme, but consumer society has long been characterized by similar combinations of local traditions and global practices. It is reasonable to critically contemplate the marriage of mass-produced doughnuts and Mohegan culture, but culture has always been dynamic and incorporated new goods and practices without simply pushing aside preexisting cultural conventions.

All consumption involves a continual process of fabricating identity, so the question we should ask of bear claws (or any other commodity) is, What do consumers take from this good and its consumption? Understood this way, consumption is a complicated social process that negotiates between dominant conditions (e.g., market economics) and our own local experiences in many distinct contexts. Food happens to be contextualized in very complicated and highly personal ways, so its meaning is particularly open to dispute—our cultural heritage, personal tastes, relationships with a marketer or brand, and nationalist sentiments are just a few of the personal factors shaping foods' symbolism. That symbolism cuts right to the heart of many dimensions of individuality, but it also exposes how we are positioned within broad market and social systems. Many of the most influential world trade systems in the last half millennium have been structured to deliver food to particular consumers. For instance, Sidney Mintz's thoughtful analysis of the sugar trade implicates sugar in class shifts in eighteenth-century Britain, dramatic changes in European colonization patterns, vast ecological transformations, and the enslavement of many Africans.[21] Tea, coffee, salt, and many other staple foods have been produced, marketed, and consumed in complex networks of laborers, retailers, and consumers who typically have no direct relationship with each other outside that product. Because laborers, marketers, and consumers are isolated and have no direct relationship outside the good itself, though, most of these structural relationships are largely unrecognized. Consumers at a local fast-food joint, for instance, normally see themselves having a quickly prepared and inexpensive burger in a convenient location; they likely do not see themselves reproducing the fabric of capitalism in a relationship with farmers, shippers, and marketers scattered all over the world. Consequently, many of us negotiate rather modest personal issues through food symbolism, yet we also are at least obliquely participants in and perhaps even critics of many of the most fundamental features of global marketing.

Many observers today believe that global standardization represented by firms like Wal-Mart conflicts with local visions of cultural distinction and identity. In this picture of global change, Ronald Mc-Donald leads a phalanx of corporate entities who collectively scorch the earth, rooting out cultural distinction and replacing it with mass-produced minutiae and radically new social organizations. From this perspective, a Big Mac brings with it a host of potentially new ways of organizing our social lives.[22] Doughnut marketers alone seem unlikely to remake the face of the planet, but they reveal the tension between, on the one hand, globalizing marketers' aspirations and, on the other, local consumers and producers. Doughnut marketers like Dunkin' Donuts and Tim Hortons have led the industry's expansion for more than half a century, and like their peers in companies such as McDonald's they have come under significant attack for disrupting communities, displacing local foods, and uprooting merchants rooted in those places.

In 1955 the newly crowned queen of National Donut Week, Nancy O'Malley, seductively posed on a bed of doughnuts. Her pinup-girl pose illuminated the desires associated with doughnuts, though her official duty was to provide "new pointers on the art of doughnut dunking." (Photograph © Bettmann/CORBIS.)

In foodways discourses the question often has been whether global marketing homogenizes local identity or is instead a heterogeneous force within which we all carve out our distinctive spaces. For example, some European food producers have banded together to oppose mass food production and consumption. The "slow food" movement, for example, aspires to protect local culinary traditions against encroaching mass-produced foods, especially American fast-food chains. Mintz argues that the United States does not really have a genuine national cuisine outside some regional dishes, so we are especially open to commercialized foodways represented by the likes of Ronald McDonald.[23] Where Americans do not have a clearly defined community who eat, cook, and ponder a distinct range of foods, Mintz argues much of the world does have such cuisines against which doughnuts and Coca-Cola are judged. The slow-food movement directly takes aim at McDonald's and fast-food marketers whose products apparently erase local culturally distinct cuisines, replacing them with the likes of hamburgers and doughnuts.

This is not to say that Americans do not share some basic foodways patterns that are quite different from much of the world. Americans, for instance, consume massive quantities of refined sugar and carbohydrates; we eat a vast volume of food cooked by other people; and our food consumption is dramatically influenced by hurry. While this serves doughnuts quite well, slow-food advocates critique global foodways' eradication of local foods and consumption patterns, arguing that a "meal has to represent a break in daily life. . . . Fast food doesn't necessarily mean eating fast, but it does mean having no time to savor what we eat and find out about its history and origin."[24] It is not by chance that the slow-food movement began in Italy; Italians have a strong tradition of regional cuisine in which family dining is an important social event, and this stands in stark contrast to the culinary experience presented by fast-food chains.

This may expose consumer culture's most fundamental dilemma: Are we empowered by consumption and goods, or are we instead willingly buying into our own oppression as we march off to Dunkin'? The picture of an evil global entity being beaten back by a host of local chefs sounds heroic, but the tension between communities and outside influences is much more complex. Inevitably, the arrival of doughnut marketers has been greeted by many different sentiments. Krispy Kreme's recent expansion into Europe, for instance, was greeted by some consumers' jubilation; people anxiously waited in a London rain for the chance to eat Krispy Kremes when the chain took up residence at Harrods in 2003. However, the chain also was attacked as yet another expansion of American slovenliness destroying local culture in pursuit of profit.

In 1998 a Canadian woman identified an image of Jesus on the wall of a Tim Hortons in Cape Breton. Crowds soon began gathering at the apparition that curiously only appeared in the evening. As pilgrims gathered and the media congregated at the phenomenon, the store's manager stressed that the odd shadow was simply a newly installed light, but the mundane explanation fell on deaf ears.[25] Nobody appeared to wonder why Jesus chose a doughnut shop for this appearance, given the warm feelings people have for doughnuts and Canadians have for Tim Hortons. One commentator agreed that "No one questioned the Son of God's choice of venue. Where else in Canada would Christ appear but at Tim Hortons?"[26] As superficially ridiculous as Jesus' appearance at Tim Hortons may be, it illuminates the significance of consumption, emphasizes the importance of apparently lowly doughnut shops, and underscores the social meaningfulness of otherwise mundane foods like doughnuts. Doughnut shops like the Cape Breton Tim Hortons are significant community spaces, yet they are spaces in which dominant economic interests commingle with local identity, momentary treats evade their impact on public health, and shows of faith blur the line between nationalism, local identity, and global capital. Food is implicated in peoples' social, economic, national, and even religious lives, and doughnuts are one of many foods weaving this complex web of relationships.

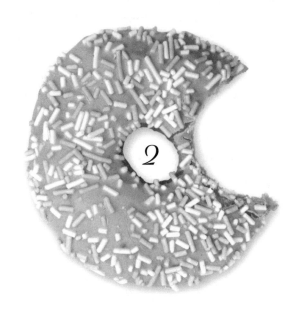

Doughnut 101: A History of Doughnuts

In 1917 the Salvation Army's Helen Purviance was among eleven young women sent to support U.S. troops in Europe, where Ensign Purviance was assigned to the American First Division.[1] The First Division was the first to embark and the last to return home, and by war's end nearly five thousand First Division members died and more than seventeen thousand were wounded. Purviance's contingent was dispatched to the Ammunition Corps in Montiers-sur-Saulx, and in August 1917 the region was hit with thirty-six consecutive days of rain in the midst of stiff combat.[2] Helen Purviance and the Salvation Army "lassies" spread the Word by running canteens, providing entertainment, and supporting troops. One of Purviance's fellow lassies acknowledged that "We know that the boys need more than sermons and songs here. They miss the care and the kindness of home and we want to give them a little of something as near like it as possible."[3] The women aspired to provide troops with something that reminded them of their homes, and they agreed that food was ideal. The women at first planned to make pies, but their camps had few reliable stoves and scarce raw materials—sugar, flour, and baking powder were the bulk of the cupboard.[4] While a couple of them tried to produce pies, Purviance began to prepare fried dough, noting that "I was literally on my knees when those first doughnuts were fried, seven at a time, in a small frying pan. There was also a prayer in my heart that somehow this home touch would do more for those who ate the doughnuts than satisfy a physical hunger."

The women's water-soaked tent collapsed on the first day of doughnut cooking, but Purviance later remembered that their first doughnuts "didn't even have time to cool before they were eaten."[5] Salvation Army women quickly began distributing doughnuts and coffee along the line, and the distinctive smell pervaded the trenches and brought

This Keystone View Company stereograph from about 1918 revealed a line of soldiers waiting for fresh doughnuts. Makeshift bakeries like this one near the Rhine were set up throughout Europe. (Photograph from author's collection.)

many more soldiers to the "Doughnut Girls." Doughnuts were sold at cost, which was six for a franc in April 1918, and even then demand outstripped supply. One soldier reported that "The Salvation Army has a nice hut where we can get real honest American cocoa, pies and doughnuts made by American girls. Gee but they taste good!" Along the trenches doughnuts became important treats that reminded soldiers of home, wives, and mothers and fortified troops in the face of war. The women were soon reportedly making as many as nine thousand doughnuts a day, and by war's end Purviance estimated that she had handed out more than a million.[6] The YMCA followed suit, delivering ten thousand doughnuts as well as another seventeen thousand packs of cigarettes to troops in Saint-Mihiel.[7] The Red Cross struck a somewhat healthier medium by serving up doughnuts and ice cream.[8] Even today the Salvation Army visits U.S. troops throughout the world and finds doughnuts remain one of soldiers' most popular treats.

The success of hot doughnuts may seem rather predictable in retrospect. Doughnuts today inspire strong emotions much like the fervor

Glazed America

they apparently generated in French trenches, and they are deeply embedded in the somewhat ambiguous entity we call American cuisine. However, doughnuts were a relatively obscure dish when Helen Purviance began frying them. Doughnuts really did not secure widespread popularity and ascend to their prominent role in American diets until the 1920s. Doughnuts are today considered a distinctly American dish throughout the world, and proponents effortlessly wrap doughnuts' symbolism in powerful nationalist sentiments, family, and faith much like that championed by the Salvation Army. Yet the doughnut's ancestry has deep historical precedents that range over the globe into antiquity, even though many of the ways in which doughnuts are made, consumed, sold, and symbolized are quite recent developments in a very lengthy pastry heritage. There may be some primal attraction to fried dough that Helen Purviance tapped into in the trenches, but the forms that dough has taken and the symbolism projected onto it have been quite wide-ranging.

Doughnut Genesis

A variety of origin myths stake the doughnut's invention anywhere from antiquity to the nineteenth century, and a wide range of cultural groups can make some claim to fried dough over that span. Fried dough certainly was born somewhere in the reaches of prehistory, but it is impossible to identify a single cultural group or region as its "inventor." The origins of the doughnut, like those of most other foods, rest in the very earliest moments of agricultural domestication, but fried dough has taken many different forms in subsequent cuisines. Some fried pastries have no tangible connection to the American doughnut that emerged around the turn of the nineteenth century, but others had a significant influence on American doughnuts.

All domesticated agricultural and animal foods can place their primordial roots in what is known as the Neolithic Revolution. Between roughly twelve thousand and ten thousand years ago, domesticated forms of emmer and einkorn wheat as well as barley began to appear in the Near East, focused in the area that is now Iraq. The intensive cultivation of plants and animals soon developed in an area ranging from present-day Israel to Turkey, and people began to live in sedentary

On February 17, 1945, the Red Cross's Deborah Bankart posed for this picture as she continued the doughnut girl tradition. During World War II she used a doughnut machine to produce pastries for soldiers stationed with the Tenth Mountain Division in Italy. (Photograph courtesy of Denver Public Library, 10th Mountain Division Resource Center Collection, Henry Moscow Collection, TMP-187.)

year-round settlements on a widespread scale for the first time. This transformation occurred more or less independently in other parts of the world, including Mesoamerica and Southeast Asia, within a few millennia with similar foods that today populate tables across the planet. Wild plants that were domesticated during this period would provide the flours that continue to be used to make doughnuts today.

Flour, the major ingredients for doughnuts, was in place from very early in this domestication process. These earliest flours looked vastly different than the multipurpose flours and doughnut flour blends that are engineered today. In antiquity stone grinding was used to reduce gathered wheat into a powder, which produced dough when water was added. Flour can be mechanically ground in many different ways, each of which produces a distinctive texture, but basic stone grinding technology remained relatively unchanged until the nineteenth century. Breads and doughnuts are typically made from wheat that varies considerably from one variety to another. Various types of wheat produce different textures based on their gluten, a protein that introduces elasticity to dough after it is kneaded. Flours with high gluten content are tougher, so they hold their form when baked into loaves, whereas cake flours are low in gluten and have a much finer texture. Early breads were eaten unleavened; that is, because they did not rise, they were flat and dense. Flour rises after the introduction of a leavening agent (such as yeast, sourdough, yogurt, or baking powder), which forces the bread to expand as carbon dioxide is produced. Egyptians began producing leavened breads by five thousand years ago, probably after the introduction of airborne yeast. Egyptians eventually introduced many different bread varieties, including a highly refined white bread that could reasonably be considered an ancestor of contemporary doughnut flours. The Greeks subsequently created an expanded range of doughs, and for the first time the Greek citizenry included laborers who made their living as bakers. Greek bakers dominated Rome's baking workforce, where the state provided bread free to citizens, and the expanding Roman Empire spread bread-making traditions throughout much of Europe.

In antiquity, flours likely were sometimes cooked in hot oils, and because oil often was a valued trade good, fried flour would have been a distinctive status food in many contexts. In some cases oil and breads became ritually linked, and there are references to oil and bread offerings in the Bible. Leviticus 7:12, for instance, indicates that a believer "shall offer with the sacrifice of thanksgiving unleavened cakes mingled with oil, and unleavened wafers anointed with oil, and cakes mingled with oil, of fine flour, fried." Many similar rituals persist today. For example, sufganiyah is a jelly doughnut traditionally served at Hanukkah. Sufganiyot commemorate the miracle of the oil following the defeat of the Greeks. A single day's oil needed to kindle the Temple Menorah miraculously lasted eight days, and during Hanukkah foods like potato latkes are fried in oil in commemoration of this event.

Olive oils, animal fats, and other vegetable oils would all have been suitable for frying various grains, and a vast range of places can make a claim to early fried treats. The Chinese probably were producing oil-fried pastries from the outset of agricultural production. During the Tang dynasty (618–907 C.E.), advances in milling techniques resulted in finer grains that were used to produce fried dough strips. Other pastry ancestors of the doughnut find their roots across Europe. Turks apparently introduced the very fine thin dough known as filo, borrowing from the Greek term *phyllo,* which is used to describe leaves. Turks used the filo dough to wrap both savory pies and sweet confections including baklava. Assyrians may have introduced baklava as early as the eighth century B.C.E., and from there it apparently traveled to Greece. Greek merchants eventually introduced it to Ottoman Turks, who engineered the form we consume today. None of this early fried dough was produced in the trademark circular form we now attach to doughnuts, but the spherical form eventually was tried in at least one place in the world. Round acorn cakes were excavated over seventy years ago in Oklahoma caves, and the cakes have the basic circular form and holes associated with doughnuts.[9] Dug by archaeologist Etienne B. Renaud, the cakes were reportedly over a thousand years old, and 1940s doughnut marketers claimed them as the world's first doughnuts.

The pairing of fried dough with sweeteners, especially sugar, was the next critical step in the evolution of the doughnut. Much of European pastry history revolves around France, where sweetened pastries became regional staples by the colonial period. French pastry techniques were initially revolutionized after the Crusaders' return from Asia in

1204. Crusaders found that cane sugar was used by a wide range of Arab and Muslim peoples. Sugar had been used in modest amounts in Europe since antiquity, but because it was rare most sweetening was done with honey or fruits. Slowly, though, new flours and more liberal use of sugar led to significant changes in pastry production. In France a guild of bakers known as oubloyers secured state privileges by 1270, producing wafers for religious holidays and everyday consumption that we would recognize as cookies. European bakers were widely using wheat flour by the thirteenth century, but they sometimes used high-grade flour to produce specialty cakes and pastries for holidays. Wealthy Europeans began to order pastries from bakers throughout the year, and soon there was widespread demand. The Paris pastry guild officially formed in 1440, producing savory pastries as well as occasional sweet pastries. In 1566 the crown officially joined the oubloyer and pastry guilds, granting them a monopoly on weddings and banquets. Increased supplies of butter and sugar, finer pastry dough, and eventually the introduction of chocolate from the New World radically expanded pastry specialization, which would reach its peak in the eighteenth and nineteenth centuries.

All of the sweet fried pastries that emerged throughout the world are relatives to the doughnut, but they are distinguished by shape, seasonings, ingredients, or preparation techniques. The northern Mexican pastry known as the sopapilla, for instance, is a flat flour crescent that can accompany a meal or be a dessert when garnished with honey, powdered sugar, or cinnamon. The German-originating bismarck often shares the contemporary bakery counter with traditional round doughnuts, but bismarcks usually are filled with jellies, although the term is now sometimes used for custard-filled pastries. Among the closest French relatives to the doughnut is the beignet, a hand-rolled, deep-fried pastry typically covered in powdered sugar. In the early eighteenth century, French migrants brought the beignet with them to New Orleans, where they became a common treat. The city's once-pricey coffee stands began to hawk less-costly coffees by the early nineteenth century, and a vast range of residents and visitors began to consume the powdery beignets with coffee. The pairing of chicory café au lait and beignets became a staple of local cuisine by the mid-nineteenth century.

Over the last half millennium foods like beignets have reflected a complex map of regional trade systems, ethnic migration patterns, and colonial expansion. Food was one of the most prized trade goods pursued by European colonizers, whose initial conquest of the globe was in large part driven by their desire to secure spices.[10] When Europeans colonized various reaches of the world, they sent indigenous foods back to their homes and introduced a vast range of European cooking techniques to their new colonial subjects. In Latin American, for instance, numerous doughnut-like foods were brought by Spanish and Portuguese colonizers. Churros are a popular Latin American fried pastry that is twisted and usually dusted with cinnamon or sugar. The Portuguese brought Brazil sonhos, an airy puff whose name translates as "dreams." Sonhos are typically dusted with sugar or cinnamon, but there are many variations that borrow the same name. The Hawaiian malassada, a sugar-coated ball of fried dough, is also a Portuguese introduction by way of the Azores. The recipe apparently came to Hawaii when Portuguese workers migrated to Hawaii in the late nineteenth century.

Some of these foodways migration stories are unpleasant reminders of the profound underside of colonization. American Indians ate something akin to what is now known as fry bread for centuries.[11] The real zenith of fry bread consumption, though, came when Europeans forced Indians onto reservations. Prohibited from gathering and hunting most traditional foods, Indians were provided with European supplies including bags of white flour. Navajos formed the flour into flat forms and cooked them in animal fats. Fry bread is typically eaten with another food like soup, or it can be filled, but it also can be sugared or covered with honey much as sopapillas. There are many contemporary versions of fry bread sold today throughout Navajo country. Cherokees likewise were displaced from ancestral homelands in the Southeast and driven to Oklahoma reservations where flour became a tool for assimilating Indians. Federal officials aspired to rid Cherokees of cultural distinctions like foodways, so they provided specific foods and taught young women mainstream cooking techniques in Indian schools. In the early twentieth century, reservation rations included flour, baking powder, sugar, and green coffee beans, the use of which was intended to meld Indians to white ways.[12] In the wake of World War II the federal government again dumped flour and lard on reservations, fanning production of fry breads and in many minds fueling epidemic obesity rates among many reservation Indians.[13]

The Dutch Dough Nut

Given all the pastries found across time, it is difficult to pinpoint the precise moment when the doughnut itself actually emerged; in fact it is not all that clear what constitutes a doughnut as distinctive from many other pastries. The very word itself often is attributed to Washington Irving, who used the word *dough nut* in his 1809 *History of New York*. Irving described stylish early colonial parties that were characterized by "more sturdy, substantial fare" than the "refinement" he associated with early-nineteenth-century New Yorkers. These gatherings witnessed massive earthen dishes "well stored with slices of fat pork, fried brown, cut up into mouthfuls, and swimming in doup [*sic*] or gravy. . . . Sometimes the table was graced with immense apple pies, or saucers full of preserved peaches and pears; but it was always sure to boast an enormous dish of balls of sweetened dough, fried in hog's fat, and called dough nuts, or oly koeks—a delicious kind of cake, at present, scarcely known in this city, except in genuine dutch families; but which retains its pre-eminent station at the tea tables in Albany."[14]

Irving's brief description of the olykoek is the first clear instance in which the doughnut and the Dutch olykoek are described as similar if not interchangeable dishes. The two-word term *dough nut* was likely in popular usage in the late eighteenth century, but it is unclear if the term was widely used or specific to particular regional or cultural groups. Sally Levitt Steinberg identified a handwritten example of the term *doughnut* among an eighteenth-century collection of Dutch recipes, so Irving and early cookbook authors were almost certainly borrowing a popularly recognized term.[15] Irving's own reference indicates that doughnuts were not commonly consumed outside "genuine dutch families," so in the early nineteenth century they may well have been a distinctive Dutch ethnic dish.

Perhaps the earliest appearance of the term in print came in Sussannah Carter's 1803 *The Frugal Housewife, or Complete Woman Cook*.[16] First published in London in 1765, Carter's well-known cookbook became one of the first cookbooks printed in America when it was republished in 1772. The 1803 edition was perhaps the first cookbook to provide a recipe for "dough nuts" to be boiled in hog's lard, just as Irving described six years later. "American cuisine" was still being defined in 1803, but *The Frugal Housewife* accorded doughnuts the status of an American dish by including them in an appendix of recipes "adapted to the American mode of cooking." The 1803 appendix was almost certainly added by English publishers eager to appeal to American readers, but the dishes in Carter's appendix do indeed sound like standards of American cuisine: Indian pudding, buckwheat cakes, pumpkin pie, maple sugar, and maple beer appear alongside the doughnut among the book's American dishes.

Most stories of the doughnut's origination point to the Dutch roots Irving championed. The Dutch olykoek's origins are wrapped in as much mystery as those of the doughnut itself, but most accounts agree that the olykoek came to America with seventeenth-century Dutch migrants.[17] Most Dutch cuisine revolved around fishing and cheeses associated with Holland's vast pasturelands, but the Dutch did prepare butter cakes and cakes spiced with ginger, cinnamon, and nutmeg. In 1669 a recipe for "Olie-koecken" appeared in a Dutch cookbook, which is perhaps the earliest printed reference to the dish.[18] However, the recipe may well have made its way to the New World earlier in the century when the Dutch colonized what is now New York. In the early seventeenth century the Dutch-directed United East India Company sent Henry Hudson to scout a northwest passage to the Indies, and in 1609 Hudson arrived in the area now known as New York and sailed up the river that today bears his name. Within two years the Dutch returned for the fur trade, and in 1624 the first Dutch immigrants arrived in the New Netherlands colony. Perhaps nine thousand residents lived in the New Netherlands in 1664, when the British took New Amsterdam.

Competing claims to the doughnut's origins stand on somewhat weaker ground than the Dutch origin tale, but other newly arrived Americans clearly brought fried dough dishes with them that may have contributed to the doughnut as it took shape in the New World. One of these claims comes from the Pilgrims, who made fried dough cakes as part of All Saints' Day. An ideologically distorted 1944 account claimed

Juan van der Hamen y Leon's *Still Life with Sweets and Pottery* (1627) includes several torus-shaped pastries in the foreground that look remarkably like the form we now associate with doughnuts. (Photograph courtesy of National Gallery of Art, Washington Samuel Kress Collection.)

that the "treasured recipe" for doughnuts came to the New World on the *Mayflower,* which explained why "to this day the citizens of Massachusetts eat more donuts than the citizens of any other state."[19] There is suggestive evidence for other European antecedents for the doughnut. Perhaps the most interesting European precedent to olykoeks and doughnuts is pointed out by Evan Jones, who notes that the 1627 Juan van der Hamen y Leon painting *Still Life with Sweets and Pottery* portrays a pair of circular pastries that are identical to what we consider doughnuts today.[20] The Spanish painter served the royal court in the 1620s, but he was the son of a Flemish courtier and could justifiably claim some Dutch heritage. Van der Hamen's 1627 work features a group of sugar-dusted pastries that were likely typical of Spanish upper-class food. However, most descriptions of the olykoek indicate that it was fried dough that was either twisted or had a nut placed in its center. Van der Hamen's painting raises the possibility that the spherical doughnut existed before a clearly defined and publicly recognized term described the pastry.

Most nineteenth- and early-twentieth-century doughnut scribes accepted that the doughnut had the Dutch origins Irving outlined. In 1899, Julian Ralph wrote that on a tour of Europe he "tracked the American doughnut to the lair from which it sprang upon our newborn nation to fasten its dyspeptic clutch upon our people. That lair is Holland. There the doughnut lurks on every hand, and, though it is not as seductive to the taste as we have learned to make it, the appearance of the creature is precisely the same."[21] The concrete difference between olykoeks and doughnuts is not entirely clear, though Ralph apparently saw both the Dutch and American versions as doughnuts in 1899 and did not use the term *olykoek*. Many earlier commentators, like Irving, seem to use the two terms interchangeably. In *Moby Dick*, for instance, Herman Melville noted that marooned Dutch whalemen referred to fried-up portions of a whale as "fritters."[22] Melville observed that these whale fritters were similar to fritters made from fried flour, "which, indeed, they greatly resemble, being brown and crisp, and smelling something like old Amsterdam housewives' dough-nuts or oly-cooks [sic], when fresh." However, other observers distinguished the Dutch version by shape or by the insertion of a nut in its center. In 1840, for example, Eliza Leslie distinguished between her "dough nuts" and olykoeks, noting that "The New York Oly Koeks are dough-nuts with currants and raisins in them."[23]

By the final decade of the nineteenth century, increasingly fewer writers made a clear distinction between doughnuts and olykoeks, and very few used the latter term at all. In 1881 *Harper's New Monthly Magazine* told the story of an "old Dutch town" that "surpassed all others in beautiful damsels, valorous young men, mince-pies, oliekoeks [sic], and New Year cookies."[24] *Harper's* nostalgia for a heroic Dutch heritage came just as the olykoek seems to have disappeared from collective memory. It is unclear if olykoeks simply disappeared or were subsumed into a doughnut tradition. The process by which olykoeks first metamorphosed into doughnuts in the eighteenth century is similarly unclear, but it probably was typical of the hybridization that takes place when multiple cuisines meet; that is, different observers and various cultural groups, regional collectives, and individual chefs produced the new doughnut form through a variety of techniques that reflect the doughnut's variant roots. In 1894 Dutch historian William Elliot Griffis argued as much, concluding that "The doughnut may have been too cosmopolitan an article to claim invention at the hands of any one people; yet what Yankee 'fried cake' or doughnut ever equaled an olekoek?"[25] As Griffis recognized, foods like doughnuts are probably typical of the hybrid dishes that characterize much of American food. Griffis understood that the United States is a distinctly polyglot country woven from numerous cultural threads that all transported various veins of what might reasonably be called American cuisine. Nevertheless, he still favored the Dutch origins, and like many subsequent food scribes he tended to paint hybridized mass American foods like the doughnut as somehow less worthy than their ethnically distinct ancestors.

The American Doughnut

Recipes for doughnuts are sprinkled throughout a series of cookbooks published around 1830, by which time many cookbook authors began to embed doughnuts within a distinctly American cuisine. Most early "American" recipes featured distinctive New World foods and were simply tacked onto Anglo-influenced cookbooks, as in Sussannah Carter's 1803 appendix. The heart of this American culinary heritage clearly descended from Anglo cookery, but by the nineteenth century Americans brought to this tradition a host of new ingredients and a distinct mix of cultural influences ranging throughout Europe and Africa. At the center of this emergent culinary tradition was Eliza Leslie, who was perhaps the most popular and widely published nineteenth-century cookbook author. First published in 1828, *Seventy-five Receipts for Pastry Cake and Sweetmeats* was the first of her nine cookbooks. Leslie staked an early claim to overt nationalism at the outset of her 1828 debut when she proclaimed that its dishes were "in every sense of the word, American."[26] Alongside her mastery of American fish, meat, and produce, Leslie included doughnut recipes leavened with "the best brewer's yeast" rather than the more rapid leavening produced by pearl ash.[27] In 1830 the anonymously authored *The Cook Not Mad* featured a series of "Good Republican [i.e., American] Dishes" that counted doughnuts among their number (and used the term "doughnut" as a single word).[28] One of the most famous cookbook authors, Lydia Marie Child, joined the rush to brand foods as American. Child first published under the pen name "the author of Hobomok" in 1824, and over her career she would write a series of well-known novels and cookbooks and perhaps secure even greater fame as one of the nation's most prominent abolitionists. In 1830 she included "dough-nuts" in the second edition of her *The Frugal Housewife*, first published a year earlier.[29] Renamed *The American Frugal Housewife* for its 1832 edition, the book eventually went through at least thirty-five editions by 1850.

Child's "dough nuts" were made with flour, sugar, eggs, butter, and pearl ash. Pearl ash was the forerunner for leavening agents like baking soda and baking powder, which were not commercially developed until Royal Baking Powder was introduced in 1835. These leavening agents would change how long it took to prepare flours, paving the way for mass production. Flour itself was changing profoundly in the mid-nineteenth century. By the second quarter of the nineteenth century most agrarian communities had mills that processed corn or wheat, but prior to the 1840s most flour was lightly milled, typically leaving the wheat germ in the flour and varying in quality from one mill to the next. In 1883 *Mrs. Lincoln's Boston Cook Book* referred to such flours as "coarse flour" that the author distinguished from a variety of mass-milled flours available to late-nineteenth-century chefs.[30] Bigger, quick-grinding milling processes emerged in the second quarter of the nineteenth century and produced a variety of very fine white flours.[31] Grain began to be produced in significant quantities throughout the Great Plains after midcentury, and entrepreneurs spent much of the third quarter of the century developing reliable transportation routes and massive mills. By the late nineteenth century this produced industrial giants like General Mills, and the marketplace was flooded by mass-produced white flours. Many of these flours were laden with a wide range of ad-

Glazed America

ditives such as baking powders and sugar. Consequently, many chefs paid close attention to their flour, and most doughnut chains today still zealously protect their flour production process and source. Factories quickly began to monopolize most production of wheat products, and the likes of Wonder Bread and Gold Medal flour were commonplace in most kitchens by 1920.[32]

More cookbook writers hailed from New England than from any other region, so much of what passed as nineteenth-century "American" cooking was largely New England cuisine. Esther Allen Howland's 1845 *The New England Economical Housekeeper* also appeared under the title *The American Economical Housekeeper* in its over forty-five years in print, and like many other broadly defined household manuals, Howland's book was a mix of recipes, household tips, and economizing morality. Howland included five doughnut recipes, one of which she termed "Economical Dough Nuts."[33] She indicated that for the economical doughnuts, "Two or three plums in each cake improve them," a comment that actually sounds a bit like olykoek descriptions. At the very least, the reference to them as "cakes" does not suggest that she envisioned a circular form. Four of her five doughnut recipes used saleratus (an early form of baking soda) as a leavening agent in place of the more impure pearl ash. The 1845 *The Housekeeper's Assistant* also used saleratus in one of its doughnut recipes, but it distinguished between "Dough Nuts" and "raised Dough Nuts." The former used saleratus, while the latter used yeast-leavened dough to be "cut in any form."[34]

Chefs steeped in a range of American cuisines began to produce ever more regional cookbooks after the middle of the nineteenth century, and many found an easy niche for doughnuts. Mary Randolph's 1824 *The Virginia Housewife* was among the first consciously regional American cookbooks, and doughnuts apparently had already found a home in southern cuisine. However, Randolph did call her doughnut recipe "Dough Nuts—A Yankee Cake," suggesting that she saw the doughnut's originations in the Northeast.[35] The recipe she outlined was in most ways no different from that in any New England–inspired cookbook, using flour, yeast, brown sugar, and butter to be made into "cakes the size of a half dollar" fried in boiling lard. In 1877, Estelle Woods Wilcox's *Buckeye Cookery* staked out a claim to a midwestern cuisine that included crullers and doughnuts. The volume recommended "clarified drippings of roast meat" as more wholesome than lard, and it counseled, "Do not eat doughnuts between April and November."[36] The recipe for "Albert's Favorite Doughnuts" noted that the dough should be rolled "to half inch in thickness, cut in rings or twists," and dried in lard, making this one of the earliest printed suggestions that doughnuts were ring-shaped. Like his midwestern neighbors, Lafcadio Hearn's well-known 1885 *La Cuisine Creole* also embraced doughnuts, including five doughnut recipes and two cruller recipes.

In 1889, *"Aunt Babette's" Cook Book* became part of the first wave of Jewish cookbooks published in the United States, following Esther Levy's 1871 *Jewish Cookery Book*. Aunt Babette included doughnuts and crullers within a rich range of kosher and nonkosher dishes. In 1897 the bilingual *Swedish-English Cookbook* also included doughnuts.[37] Seven years later, *The Blue Grass Cook Book* brought together the southern border state's cuisine and included several doughnut recipes, one of which even had whisky among its ingredients.[38] The position doughnuts readily assumed within early regional cookbooks indicates that they were rapidly integrated into many different culinary traditions, despite their Yankee and Dutch roots.

The Linguistics and Geometry of Fried Dough

Much of the nineteenth-century discussion about doughnuts and fried relatives like crullers reflected distinct regional and social naming conventions that would slowly erode in the face of twentieth-century mass production. These naming conventions for various forms of fried dough were mirrored by variations in the shapes doughnuts assumed and their basic preparation. Many of the regional culinary variations revolved around the distinction between doughnuts and crullers. Like the doughnut, the cruller is sometimes attributed to the Dutch, and Washington Irving again provides one of the earliest mentions of crullers. In the 1819 "Legend of Sleepy Hollow," Irving described a Dutch table at which there was "the doughty doughnut, the tender olykoek, and the crisp and crumbling cruller; sweet cakes and short cakes, ginger cakes and honey cakes, and the whole family of cakes." There likely were regional naming and cooking variations for these pastries from the outset. Henry David Thoreau, for example, described his host's response when Thoreau left a New England breakfast in 1865: "Finally, filling our pockets with doughnuts, which he was pleased to find that we called by the same name that he did . . . we took our departure."[39] This suggests that in at least some mid-nineteenth-century circles doughnuts and other pastries were being defined in regionally distinct forms, likely with some distinctive preparation and materials as well.

Crullers have their own origination myths distinct from those of doughnuts, and like later doughnut origin tales the cruller's story eventually was attributed to a single inventor. In 1894 William Elliot Griffis detailed the most popular Dutch cruller genesis tale. Griffis boasted, "Was not cruller . . . first brought to perfection by Captain Kroll (pronounced and sometimes spelled crull), the whilom commander and Dutch church elder at Fort Orange?" A 1926 *New York Times* account repeated this story that the doughnut's "variant, the cruller, was one of the first Dutch inventions in New Amsterdam, achieved by an early city father and church elder, Sebastian Krol, for whom the product was named."[40] Krol, a founding member of the New Netherland congregation in 1628, was described in Griffis's 1909 *The Story of New Netherland* as "a church elder, a comforter of the sick, and one of the shining characters of New Netherland. To him is ascribed the cruller, or Krol-yer, a toothsome delicacy of high repute. The word is unknown in Holland, and the makers of dictionaries have vainly endeavored to derive the word from the Dutch, or German *krullen*, to curl. When provisions were short, or the bill of fare at Fort Orange was monotonous, Captain Krol supplied a new sort of *olekoek*, that is, 'fried cake,' 'doughnut,' or compound of flour, eggs, butter, and sugar. Krol, with his 'erollers' [*sic*], added a new delicacy to the frontier table."[41] The evidence is certainly not overwhelming, and many of these early food histories tended to seek out individual inventors for dishes and avoid the anthropologically complicated ground of tracing a food's origins into a dynamic multiethnic past. However, if Krol introduced the cruller in the first half of the seventeenth century then something approximating the doughnut may have been produced well over a century before it appears in any primary texts.

Irving's "Legend of Sleepy Hollow" distinguishes between doughnuts, crullers, and olykoeks as separate dishes, which complicates his earlier reference to doughnuts and olykoeks as essentially interchangeable pastries. However, most early references to these three foods also seem to distinguish between them as Irving did in "Sleepy Hollow." For instance, Sussannah Carter's 1803 cookbook includes crullers and doughnuts separately in its appendix of American dishes. Carter's doughnuts were formed from a pound of flour, a quarter pound of butter, a quarter pound of sugar, and two spoonfuls of yeast, all of which were mixed together in milk or water prior to being placed in boiling hog's lard. Her crullers used a pound of flour, half a pound of butter, and "half a pound of good brown-sugar," all of which were also fried in hog's lard. Carter gave identical instructions for shaping doughnuts and crullers alike: "make them into what form you please." In 1831 *The Cook Not Mad*'s recipe for crullers noted that they were "sometimes called Miracls [*sic*] or Wonders," the latter a term repeated in 1840 in Eliza Leslie's *Directions for Cookery*. However, this usage does not appear to have been very widely embraced (at least by cookbook authors), and recipes for olykoeks do not appear in cookbooks after the mid-nineteenth century.

Regional doughnut variations emerged relatively quickly. For instance, Estelle Woods Wilcox's 1877 *Buckeye Cookery* hearkened back to the region's frontier heritage when it argued that "Crullers are better the day after they are made."[42] Because food needed to be stored for long periods and fresh ingredients were not especially easy to obtain, some frontier chefs favored crullers. Sounding a call that continues to reverberate among doughnuts fans today, Eliza Leslie agreed that doughnuts "should be eaten quite fresh, as next day they will be tough and heavy; therefore it is best to make no more than you want for immediate use."[43] Unlike her yeast-risen doughnuts, Eliza Leslie's crullers were placed into boiling lard and covered with sugar, producing a confection that "will keep a week or more." However, one account of life in the Klondike celebrated doughnuts' preservation, indicating that "doughnuts are all-important to the man who goes on trail for a journey of any length. Bread freezes easily, and there is less grease and sugar, and hence less heat in it, than in doughnuts. The latter do not solidify except at extremely low temperatures, and they are very handy to carry in the pockets of a Mackinaw jacket and munch on as one travels on. They are made much after the manner of their brethren in warmer climes, with the exception that they are cooked in bacon grease—the more grease, the better."[44]

In 1895, the journal *Dialect Notes* assessed the regionally distinctive terms for doughnuts and provided the first systematic etymology for the term *doughnut*. It identified three basic varieties of doughnuts that were known by "various names in different localities" and indicated that "the only thing known as doughnuts . . . in W. Conn." was dough-nuts "raised with yeast, sweetened and spiced; generally cut in cubes and forming a roundish lump after puffing out in frying." The second type of doughnut was "raised with yeast, unseasoned; sweetened; cut in rings or twisted." This type of doughnut was called "*biled-cakes* if in twisted form, and *jumbles* if in rings." This stereotypically ring-shaped doughnut with hole was known under the same name we use today "On Cape Cod, and generally in Eastern Mass." To complicate the distinction between crullers and doughnuts, the analysis indicated that in "the Dutch-settled districts the word *olykoeks*, which Washington Irving has made classic, is used for some of the varieties. *Crullers* is also common." This complicated etymology suggests that in some circles the terms *cruller, doughnut,* and even *olykoek* were still used interchangeably at the end of the nineteenth century. To make things even more confusing, a third type of doughnut was "raised with yeast, unseasoned; merely dough from the regular batch of bread, fried instead of baked; eaten hot, with molasses." In some regions this sort of doughnut "was called simply *fried bread*." These fried bread, yeast-raised doughnuts sometimes "are known as '*seventy-fours*'—for what reason is unknown, unless, as a young friend once suggested, it is 'because you have to eat seventy-four of them to get breakfast.'" At the end of this etymology the journal admitted that a "full account of the naming of the various kinds [of doughnuts] in various sections would be interesting."[45]

Some of the regional variations in the distinction between crullers and doughnuts persisted into the twentieth century. For instance, according to the *New York Times,* doughnut defenders were aghast in 1907 when Sweden's Prince Wilhelm visited the United States and "while sitting on a high stool in the railroad restaurant at Pittsfield, Mass., ate doughnuts. But did he? The testimony comes from New England, and in the manner of doughnuts that part of this country has never been orthodox." The *Times* was concerned that Wilhelm had actually been served a cruller, because "Up in Maine they call a cruller a doughnut; and in Massachusetts their comprehension of a doughnut is uncertain." The paper drew inspiration from Washington Irving, who "knew the doughnut well, and described it as a round ball of sweetened dough, fried in hog's fat. Our Dutch ancestors esteemed it at its solid worth. A doughnut contains some yeast, or in these degenerate days, baking powder. It is soft and spongy. On the other hand, the cruller is made with eggs, and consists of shortened dough twisted around a hole. A cruller is crisp and 'short' as a good Welsh rabbit. . . . We sadly fear Prince Wilhelm ate a cruller or two at Pittsfield, and will carry the memory of them back to Sweden to the detriment of the great Republic."[46]

Much disagreement over the definition of doughnuts and crullers has suggested that the true distinction is the shape of the two pastries. In 1916, for instance, C. P. Benedict remembered "crullers twisted and with holes when I first came to New York in 1854." He did not remember the circular doughnut form, instead characterizing his 1840s childhood New England doughnuts as "larger than a goose egg and about the same shape."[47] However, Sussannah Carter's 1803 distinction between crullers and doughnuts apparently did not rest on their shape, and most pastry aficionados distinguish crullers as dough leavened with baking powder, or, prior to mass-produced baking powders, with baking soda.[48] Some subsequent commentators have suggested that crullers are identical dough that is simply cut into thin, stretched strips as opposed to circles or rounded balls.[49]

A survey of cookbooks over most of the nineteenth century suggests that there was relatively little concern with the doughnut's final form, though some cookbooks may not have been especially accurate reflections of how most cooks were producing doughnuts. Mary Randolph's 1824 doughnuts were made with brown sugar, flour, milk, and yeast and formed into "cakes the size of a half dollar."[50] The 1805 American version of Hannah Glasse's *The Art of Cookery* indicated chefs should make their doughnuts in "what form you please."[51] In *Seventy-five Receipts*, Eliza Leslie decreed that her doughnuts should be "cut into diamonds" and covered with sugar.[52] Her 1837 *Directions for Cookery, in Its Various Branches* reproduced her advice to "cut into thick diamond shapes," but no other cookbook authors apparently considered doughnuts appropriately triangular.[53] Leslie counseled that her "Wonders, or Crullers" should be cut into "long slips with a jagging iron, or with a sharp knife, and twist them into various fantastic shapes."[54] In 1885 Lafcadio Hearn echoed Leslie's advice on shaping crullers when he indicated they should be "cut in fancy shapes."[55] Hearn indicated that his yeastless doughnuts "may be made in rings and fried," whereas he counseled that the sour-milk doughnuts should be cut in no defined form.[56] Likewise, his "plain" doughnuts were simply intended to be "cut into shapes."[57] In 1889, *Aunt Babette's" Cook Book* championed an unusual shape for doughnuts, instructing cooks to "Cut a slit about an inch long in the center of each [three-inch-long dough] strip, and pull one end through this slit."[58] Aunt Babette instructed chefs that their crullers should be "cut into fanciful shapes."[59]

One somewhat overwrought doughnut defender signing her letter as "Grandma" wrote to the *New York Times* in 1913 that "Next to militant suffragettes nothing so convinces me of the degeneracy of our times as the groping ignorance of your correspondents who write about doughnuts and crullers."[60] "Grandma" argued that doughnuts are raised with yeast, so they take longer to prepare, but crullers are raised quickly with sour milk and soda, or baking powder. She argued that the shape itself was relatively unimportant and hinted that doughnuts were somehow more noble than crullers because they required more work by a chef. Another respondent sounded a similar aspersion, agreeing that "The doughnut is born of leisure and forethought, the 'child of silence and slow time,' being raised with yeast, set in sponge over night behind the kitchen stove, kneaded in the morning and left to rise again before being fried." In contrast, "The cruller is a creature of impulse, quickly stirred together, raised with baking powder or its equivalent, and fried upon the spur of the moment. The doughnut is the nobler nutriment, and was the fare of the Pilgrims."[61]

Finding the Doughnut Hole

In 1937 the community of Bangor, Maine, gathered to memorialize one of their own, Captain Hanson Gregory, who is often considered the "inventor" of the doughnut hole.[62] A variety of origin myths championed by twentieth-century doughnut promoters and Gregory himself link the former sailor and his family to the doughnut hole. Hanson, whose headstone records 1921 as the year of his death, reportedly went to sea as a young man and spent some of his time as a cook. During that tenure, according to one version, he was said to have lamented his oceangoing fried fare, because "a doughnut was just a square chunk of dough fried in fat. For the most part doughnuts were soggy, greasy and almost indigestible. Naturally sea-going folk called them 'sinkers.'" Gregory reportedly made changes in his ingredients to no avail before he asked himself, "'Why so much dough in one lump?' He got a tin-smith to make an implement that cut the dough into rings, leaving the famous hole in the middle." For this innovation Hanson was nominated to the National Doughnut Hall of Fame, which declared that he "not only discovered the hole in the first place, but invented the proper process for enclosing the hole in the doughnut."[63]

According to another Gregory family origins tale, Hanson's mother, Elizabeth, removed the centers from her olykoeks and filled them with hazelnuts, and some observers argue this explains the term "dough-nut."[64] Since Washington Irving had used the term *doughnut* a half century earlier, Elizabeth's claim to naming the doughnut seems infeasible, but she may still have had a role in her son's innovation. One account argues that she provided her son a haul of hazelnut-filled doughnuts for a sea trip in 1847, but Hanson found steering the boat was impossible while eating a doughnut (a complaint familiar to many contemporary drivers). Consequently he drove the pastries through the ship's wheel, yielding the familiar torus we now call a proper doughnut. A modestly more feasible tale holds that Gregory's mother borrowed spices like nutmeg and cinnamon from her son's cargo and added lemon rinds so that the pastries might store over a long voyage and have some scurvy-resistant qualities.[65] Although it seems unlikely that doughnuts could effectively ward off scurvy, Gregory himself apparently backed up his family's link to the doughnut in turn-of-the-century interviews.[66]

In 1940 a group met in New York to assess Gregory's claim to the doughnut hole in what they heralded as the "Great Doughnut Debate."[67] Hanson Gregory's descendants showed up to champion their ancestor's claim, and a report pored over primary documents that backed Gregory's claim to the doughnut hole. The report ruled for Gregory and spun a somewhat new origin tale, concluding that "Young Hanson was in the

Glazed America

kitchen of his home watching his mother make fried cakes. He asked her why the centers got so soggy. She said that for some reason they never got cooked. Then the boy decided to poke out the center of some uncooked cakes with a fork. His mother cooked them. They were the first (ring) doughnuts."[68]

Much of this "debate" over the doughnut's origins (or at least the hole's origins) did not emerge until the 1930s, when it was orchestrated by the doughnut champions at the Doughnut Corporation of America. It is unclear why they championed Gregory's claim, but there likely was a certain appeal to placing the doughnut's origin with a New England seafarer. By the 1930s the doughnut had some relatively widely accepted roots in New England foodways. In 1918, for example, the *Cleveland Advocate* reported from wartime France that "every fighter over here might have been born in New England, where they eat 'em for breakfast, so pronounced is the reverence for the great American doughnut."[69] Gregory gave that heritage an individual inventor for its face.

The Breakfast Doughnut

By the time the Salvation Army lassies were producing doughnuts in World War I France, the ring-shaped doughnut apparently was being consumed in many American homes. There is no clear evidence that doughnuts were at that point considered a breakfast food, with doughnut consumption being noted in a vast range of settings and at various times of day. Washington Irving's earliest reference to doughnuts came in a description of Dutch parties that "commonly assembled at three o'clock, and went away about six."[70] In 1865 Henry David Thoreau described a Cape Cod breakfast at which "we had eels, buttermilk cake, cold bread, green beans, doughnuts, and tea," but many other Americans did not restrict doughnuts to their morning meals or have especially clear codes for the foods with which doughnuts should be eaten.[71] In 1878 Harriet Beecher Stowe described an evening "supper of pork-and-beans and doughnuts," which in retrospect seems to rival Thoreau's breakfast pairing of eels and doughnuts.[72] In 1859 Seba Smith recounted being prepared for a long trip by his mother, who "fried me some doughnuts and put 'em into a box along with some cheese and sausages."[73] Consequently, nineteenth-century doughnuts appear to have been an especially flexible food capable of conforming to many different meals and contexts. As late as World War II the Doughnut Corporation of America's promotional literature still included three pages of advice on how to consume doughnuts with any meal from morning until bedtime.

Many diners clearly consumed doughnuts throughout the day. Elinore Pruitt Stewart described an 1847 dinner that included "twelve large loaves of the *best* rye bread; a small tub of doughnuts; twelve coffee-cakes, more to be called fruitcakes, and also a quantity of little cakes with seeds, nuts, and fruit in them."[74] A lengthy 1876 obituary remembered that the deceased "used to get up at daylight, breakfast sparingly, and trudge off to Santa Clara with a lunch of doughnuts in his pocket prepared by his landlady."[75] Bertha M. Woods's 1922 *Foods of the Foreign-Born in Relation to Health* noted in its section on Hungarians that a typical Hungarian field worker's Sunday supper included "doughnuts with jelly inside," which shared the table with "fried meat from soup," mashed potato, "bread (rye)," fruit, wine, and whisky.[76]

Other consumers found their doughnuts at the breakfast table. For instance, before ascending the gallows in Northampton, Massachusetts, in 1886, the condemned Allan Adams requested a last breakfast of "meat pie, crackers, tea, and doughnuts."[77] Doughnuts' emergence as a breakfast food appears to have begun in the 1920s, when they appeared on a handful of restaurant menus. In 1919, for instance, the menu for the Venice Cafeteria in Venice, California, included "homemade doughnuts" for three cents on its breakfast menu alongside many of the foods we now take as staple breakfast items: waffles, ham, eggs, sausage, cereal, and fruit juices.[78] In 1921 Utah's *Davis County Clipper* outlined its advice for "hot weather" breakfasts and indicated that a "slice or two of bacon or slivers of broiled ham with toast and an egg, if desired, a cup of coffee or milk, with or without a cooky [*sic*] or doughnut, makes a very satisfactory meal for the average person."[79] In 1932 a New York soda and candy shop advertised a choice of "whole wheat or jelly doughnuts" as part of its breakfast menu.[80]

Federal nutrition standards established during World War II could have wounded doughnut sales as the government championed healthy foods and began to view breakfast as a significant meal. Kellogg's, for instance, greeted the standards as a potential boon, because "coffee and roll" consumers could be induced to begin eating whole-grain cereals.[81] Rationing and food conservation made adherence to federal standards impractical, though, and the government could not seem to overcome the pervasive advertising of food manufacturers. What a "typical" breakfast included remained relatively flexible. In 1959, Secretary of Agriculture Ezra Taft Benson appeared at a Cologne promotion with doughnut salesman Richard Mullins to promote American breakfast foods. The *New York Times* reported that Benson "loyally sipped California and Florida orange juice, ate a patty of United States–grown rice curry and munched one of Mr. Mullins' doughnuts."[82]

Doughnuts as Mass Commodities

Doughnut marketing and consumption were radically transformed by two periods of social and material change in the twentieth century. The first came in the 1920s, when doughnut marketing became the mass phenomenon we understand it to be today. Broad marketing shifts and changes in consumers' income, leisure time, and even philosophical sentiments toward shopping contributed to dramatic changes in the American consumer landscape. In some historians' minds, this is the moment that America became a mass consumer culture in which consumption and material desire became the heart of Americans' citizen identity.[83] At this very moment doughnuts began to be mass-produced, inexpensively available in a wide range of outlets, and marketed by centralized producers who standardized supplies and doughnut production machinery. This rather sudden movement of doughnut production from households to public mass production was mirrored by shifts in other industries that also became radically streamlined as they hawked goods to a rapidly expanding consumer audience. Assembly lines had been part of American labor in some industries since the nineteenth century, but at the start of the twentieth century they had their most profound impact in the auto industry. Henry Ford's embrace of assembly-line mass production, the focus on production efficiency, and his commitment to bring mass-produced goods to vast consumer constituencies had a significant impact outside auto manufacturing. Many of the fast food marketers who emerged between the 1930s and 1950s transported much of the logic of an auto assembly line to food production, and car culture itself was essential to the growth of the fast-food industry.[84]

These 1920s shifts laid the foundation for the doughnut's increased popularity and second period of change in the wake of World War II. For many Americans, the 1920s promise of a mass consumer bounty was denied by economic marginality and social peripheralization. Although the decade did deliver cheap vaudeville shows, occasional vacations, and modest consumer goods like doughnuts, it did not provide a mountain of commodities or outrageous riches. In the late 1940s and 1950s, though, an affluent postwar America was able to secure much of the material prosperity that 1920s consumer culture had promised. Persistent income disparities in the 1920s had maintained distinct class differences between prosperous and working-class Americans, but after World War II the lot of working people improved significantly and made many of the consumer dreams of the 1920s truly accessible. Many families now could reasonably set their sights on a newly defined American dream that placed suburban home ownership at its heart. With GI Bill support, veterans led the charge to newly constructed suburbs throughout the country, and federal mortgage programs made the same suburban home ownership accessible to other working people.

The postwar charge to the suburbs came behind the wheel of the automobile as cars and an expanding roadway system became the glue holding together community space. The birth of a residential periphery accessed by car spawned a vast number of retail strips leading to and from urban centers. Marketers competing for commuting consumers' dollars sold many different sorts of inexpensive foods ranging from hamburgers to fried chicken to doughnuts. The low cost of these foods reflected standardized production techniques and raw materials that were often supplied by centralized franchisers or producers. It was in these spaces that fast-food chains including doughnut shops exponentially increased and radically changed the way Americans ate.

The transformation of food marketing from 1920s to the Cold War is clearly documented in the story of the fabled root beer franchise A&W. The A&W chain was typical of the fast-food franchisers who rapidly began to market to mobile consumers and really prospered with the

In 1940 Beryl Holmquist posed with the "Commuter's Friend" at the Congress of American Inventors meeting in Los Angeles. The contraption permitted a diner to read the newspaper while one's doughnuts were automatically dunked. (Photograph © Bettmann/CORBIS.)

emergence of roadside retail strips. A&W was first sold in a California roadside stand in 1919, and in 1923 the operation expanded to several curbside service stands near Sacramento that are sometimes considered the first "drive-in" service.[85] By the middle of the depression the chain had about two hundred stores with prominent signs that featured a trademarked bull's-eye logo. The chain sold root beer syrup to franchisees, so it was a technically straightforward operation, and the only food the stores sold consistently was hot dogs. The small, inexpensive roadside stores were well suited to suburbanization, and after the war the number of stores increased to about four hundred.

This strategy of selling inexpensive standardized food along the road to car-bound consumers was a significant shift from the way food was being made and consumed before World War I, and it was a transformation that involved doughnut marketing. Some turn-of-the-century bakeries produced doughnuts, but typically this was a sideline that left much doughnut production to households. In 1920, though, doughnuts were already an annual $20 million business nationwide, so the subsequent 1920s expansion of doughnut consumption did not simply spring from nowhere.[86] A 1921 study indicated that doughnuts selling for 5 cents cost lunchroom proprietors 1.03 cents each, so high-volume doughnut sales could garner good profits.[87] Still, most doughnuts were apparently being sold in "sit-and-sip" urban lunchrooms, with roadside sales still more than a decade away.

The increased popularity of doughnuts following World War I is sometimes attributed to doughboys who evangelized for the cause on their return, and the Salvation Army's wartime service did have an effect on doughnuts' public symbolism. In 1919, for instance, returning doughboys were taken to Coney Island, with "the Salvation Army busily engaged in handing out doughnuts."[88] The *New York Times* even hinted at mixed feelings toward the Salvation Army's adoption of the doughnut, suggesting that a "reader could feel his bitter attitude toward the organization that had made the doughnut its own, taken it to its bosom, as it were, and adapted it for a sign and a symbol. And yet how those doughboys took to those doughnuts!" This suggests that at least some observers saw the doughnut as a nationally held commodity whose symbolism was appropriately defined by the public and not businesses or even a benevolent organization like the Salvation Army.

This is a modest but telling insight into how consumers have often felt about certain popular commodities that become part of our shared social symbolism.

Despite the Salvation Army's elevation of doughnut symbolism in public consciousness, the mechanization of doughnut production was probably the single most critical shift in 1920s doughnut marketing and consumption. Subsequent shifts in how doughnuts were mass-marketed were also dependent on the mechanization of doughnut production, so this was an essential first step in doughnuts' ascension to mass-consumed good. Perhaps the most influential player was Russian immigrant Adolph Levitt, who arrived in the United States from what was then Bulgaria in the 1890s. When Levitt arrived in the country he ran a chain of Wisconsin department stores.[89] In 1916 he followed the trail of many ambitious entrepreneurs and went to New York City, where he bought into a bakery chain. His granddaughter indicates that Levitt was among the marketers who were impressed by the troops' fondness for doughnuts, so Levitt stepped up production of doughnuts in his Harlem bakery.[90] The former department store impresario understood the value of marketing theater, so he moved a kettle to the bakery's display window. However, Levitt also was vexed by what many bakers disliked about doughnut production: frying vast numbers of doughnuts in hot oil was unpleasant work requiring bakers to patiently shape doughnuts, stand over a hot kettle, and fan away fumes during the frying process. Perhaps more importantly, the crowds who gathered for Levitt's window production show appeared willing to buy many more doughnuts than he could prepare by hand.

Bakers had already tried a variety of partial mechanization processes to minimize their production time and address dilemmas like spattering and fumes, and Levitt joined their number. He enlisted an engineer to help him produce a doughnut-making machine, and in 1920 they developed a working prototype that was installed in Levitt's Harlem window and marketed to other bakers. The *New York Times* already had advertisements in 1920 seeking salesmen "to carry doughnut machines, [as a] sideline; those calling on baker trade preferred."[91] A clever marketer, Levitt began hawking doughnut machines and prepared flour mixes all over the country. Like many of his marketing peers, he recognized that bakery and product standardization had the potential to

At Long's Bakery in south Indianapolis, yeast doughnuts make the march toward glazing in the largely automated contemporary production process. (Photograph courtesy of Wade Terrell Tharp.)

make his enterprise quite successful, and his once-local doughnut shop soon mushroomed into additional stores that reached outside New York.

Levitt's chain was called Mayflower Doughnuts, borrowing one of the most prominent nationalist symbols for his brand. Levitt founded the Doughnut Corporation of America, which became a tireless commercial promoter of doughnuts. Their National Donut Month was first celebrated in October 1928, and the Doughnut Corporation flooded marketers with point-of-sale counsel and mounted intensive advertising campaigns in print media, radio, and eventually television. With a shop on Times Square, Levitt leveraged significant publicity and had Hollywood stars and starlets campaigning for the Dunking Association.

However, Levitt's most important move may have been the standardization of doughnut machines and the marketing of prepared doughnut supplies that he could sell to other doughnut-shop operators. This sort of standardization and streamlining eventually became standard organization among chains, so Levitt was clearly at the forefront of a revolution in how doughnuts and other fast foods could be mass-produced and -consumed. Bakers often complained that their flour supplies were unpredictable, and even with a reliable flour source bakers often spent significant amounts of time mixing flour to get the correct consistency. Introducing premixed ingredients was a key change that allowed for more uniform products, speeded the manufacture process, and allowed for semiskilled laborers to produce doughnuts. With bags of prepared flour, a shop could simply dump a bag into a mixer and add ingredients, so the production did not require the accomplished decision-making skills of a trained baker. Levitt was not alone in his effort to streamline doughnut manufacturing. In Michigan, Eugene Worden and Grover Levy had successful bakeries in Jackson and Lansing. The partners began selling preblended doughnut flour to other bakers, licensing its use to doughnut makers throughout the country. However, contrary to the belief that the doughnut business was depression-proof, Worden and Lutz were leveled by the depression and sold their businesses.

One of the key challenges to creating a doughnut mix was concocting a preparation that needed only water to produce the dough and did not require egg yolks. Levitt turned to a New Jersey importer, Joe Lowe, who suggested using dried egg yolk powder from China. Levitt took Lowe's advice but bolted to secure a cheaper yolk powder than Lowe supplied, so Lowe and partner Louis Price began producing doughnut-making equipment in addition to the ice cream supplies the Joe Lowe Corporation had sold since 1909.[92] Lowe's company purchased the rights to the Popsicle from its San Francisco inventor in 1925, and Price's son Harold joined the firm in 1928 and established Cottage Donuts in 1938.[93] Meanwhile, Levitt expanded his operation and was likely selling doughnut machines in Canada by 1931.[94] In 1935 his representatives set up what became known as the Canadian Doughnut Company, and the Canadian affiliate's innovations mirrored those of its American parent company. By the end of World War II the Doughnut Corporation of America was the world's largest maker of doughnut mixes and bakery goods, with a massive Maryland mill. The company also had established factories in Canada, England, and Australia and built a five-story New York City laboratory dedicated to "elaborate apparatus that tests every step in the making of this once lowly fried cake."[95]

Levitt possessed a creative marketing mind, but the doughnut's emergence was especially well timed. In the 1920s foods became increasingly less expensive, with most American households spending far less on food than they ever had before. This was in many ways the culmination of more than half a century of growth in industrialized food production that increased supplies and decreased costs. Increasingly more food was being eaten outside the home, an evolving result of decreased food prices, increasing personal incomes, and urban commuting that encouraged the growth of rapid-service restaurants like soda fountains and cafés.[96] Apparently the helpings were larger, too, because a 1928 study showed that on the eve of the depression Americans were consuming two pounds more each day than they had in 1914.[97] Those foods, though, were laden with vastly more sugar than ever before, and in the 1920s heart attacks overtook tuberculosis as Americans' most common cause of death. While this would have significant long-term implications on public health, doughnuts played well into the nation's increasingly powerful sweet tooth.

Impressionistic data suggest that the depression did not hurt doughnut sales, since they were so cheap that their consumption con-

The popularity of Al Capone's 1930 soup line may have been connected to his offering of free doughnuts. "Big Al's Kitchen for the Needy" provided about thirty-five hundred people a day with meals of soup, bread, coffee, and doughnuts. (Photograph © Bettmann/CORBIS.)

tinued relatively unabated. If anything, some observers argue, the depression actually expanded doughnut consumption. Adolph Levitt's granddaughter Sally Levitt Steinberg voices the common argument that doughnut consumption tends to provide an inverse mirror of the nation's broader economy, because doughnuts are usually most profitable and common when the economy is doing poorly.[98] Manufacturers have recurrently been compelled to cut dough usage during moments of economic stress and wartime, but doughnuts are inexpensive and filling foods that might reasonably flourish in the face of penury. In 1929 Americans consumed 216 million doughnuts, though estimates of doughnut consumption are notoriously problematic and bakers often will make smaller doughnuts to stretch their supplies.[99] The Doughnut Corporation of America's own data indicate that doughnuts increased in popularity from the depression through the war, with U.S. consumption rising from 1.26 billion doughnuts in 1933 to 3.96 billion in 1939. Whether that increase was a direct reflection of the broader economy is unclear, because with the war nearing its end in 1945, that number had nearly doubled yet again, to 7.2 billion.[100] Today by one count roughly 10 billion doughnuts are consumed each year in the United States.[101]

Doughnuts and Car Culture

In the mid-1950s, Dunkin' Donuts founder William Rosenberg made a cross-country trip to survey other doughnut shops as he contemplated expanding his already successful chain. The Massachusetts native found that "only in California did we see a lot of drive-in donut stores, because in places like that, they didn't have streetcars; it was all automobile traffic."[102] Indeed, many of Rosenberg's New England shops were in compact communities still far less attached to cars than their California counterparts, so he had not really contemplated the relationship between car commuting and doughnut consumption. However, Rosenberg quickly recognized the significance of commuting patterns on doughnut sales, and Dunkin' began to closely assess their earliest shops' locations with an eye toward traffic visibility and access. At one potential shop site, Rosenberg and his son "stood and counted the traffic flow (how many cars passed by in a minute)" and examined factors including "accessibility, visibility, and traffic count."[103] Little did Rosenberg know that this process of examining traffic flow, parking, and visibility and placing doughnut shops in the midst of commuter routes would become a science in coming years as chains developed strict methods for assessing franchise locations.[104]

A variety of cafés, soda counters, cafeterias, and diners were serving relatively quickly prepared foods to American diners in the early twentieth century, but the number of these venues mushroomed as the car transformed American urban space from the 1920s onward.

Installment buying was introduced to automobile purchasing in 1915, and it witnessed rapid growth in the 1920s while the American road system began to slowly expand. However, this did not place cars in every American's garage, and most households ended the 1920s without an automobile. By the outset of World War II about half of American urbanites were still without a car, and most Americans were still renting.[105] The desire to own a car and home was commonplace, though, and this paired ambition gradually moved to the heart of American consumer expectations. Following the war, home and car ownership became the norm, reshaping cities and transforming fast-food marketing, including doughnut sales.

Roadside stands like A&W and many smaller seasonal operations—the precursors to roadside fast-food chains—were serving convenience food to travelers in the 1920s. Doughnut shops never really flourished along roads serving long-distance travelers, though, because doughnuts turned out to be a shorter-distance commuter food. The models for commuter food venues were drive-in restaurants that dated back to at least 1921, when Royce Hailey's Pig Stand opened in Dallas.[106] As William Rosenberg recognized, most of the early drive-throughs emerged in postwar California, where an extensive freeway system served numerous suburban towns that spread over vast spaces with no real urban center.[107] Harry and Esther Snyder's In-N-Out Burger opened a drive-through with speaker in 1948 and Jack in the Box followed in 1951, though industry behemoth McDonald's did not join them until 1975.[108]

Much of America would soon look more like California. Between 1950 and 1980 the number of American cars increased by 200 percent, while the population increased by just half.[109] Peripheral subdivisions sprang up throughout postwar America, producing many lower-density, socially homogeneous cookie-cutter communities throughout the country. Canadian car ownership likewise doubled between 1945 and 1952, and at least one Canadian doughnut maker had installed a drive-through in 1959.[110] This suburbanization created more commuters, and small marketers sprung up along commuting strips outside urban centers.[111] These changes paved the way for gas stations, chain restaurants, and doughnut shops, all of which were ideally suited to drive-through sales. For commuters, small, filling, and inexpensive

Among the best-known and most recognizable doughnut shops in the world is Randy's Donuts in Inglewood, California. Built in 1953, Randy's was originally part of the Big Donut Drive-In chain, which featured massive doughnuts atop otherwise commonplace fast-food spaces. The massive steel doughnut was typical of the 1950s roadside architecture geared toward capturing commuters' attention. Well known for its twenty-two-foot-diameter steel doughnut, Randy's has appeared in a Snoop Doggy Dog video, movies (including *Earth Girls Are Easy*), and numerous television shows. (Photograph courtesy of Gary L. Friedman, www.FriedmanArchives.com.)

doughnuts were an especially good fit with car consumption, and marketers found that doughnuts could be made inexpensively in almost any retail space through which consumers passed.

Fueled by mass-produced ingredients, doughnut machines, and the growth of car culture, a host of doughnut chains came of age after World War II. Doughnut machines and ingredients are not especially costly, doughnut shops are not very large, and the manufacturing process is straightforward, so establishing a doughnut shop is relatively inexpensive. Chains made this even more systematic, providing their franchisees with ingredients, equipment, accounting systems, and marketing campaigns. The first restaurant chains emerged in the 1920s, including restaurants like White Castle and White Tower that provided a narrow range of foods hawked from standardized buildings.[112] Other chains, led by Howard Johnson's, focused on the emergent roadway system and eventually provided counter and booth service alike for meals and the chain's trademark ice cream.[113] Most early chains were regionally focused, and doughnut franchises would follow this pattern.

A stream of long-lived doughnut chains emerged around World War II. Among the best-known today is Krispy Kreme, which was established by Vernon Rudolph in 1937. In Krispy Kreme lore, Rudolph purchased a Kentucky doughnut shop in 1933 and received the shop and its doughnut recipe, which was reputedly secured from a French chef. Rudolph's family ran a wholesale operation selling doughnuts to groceries in the Nashville area, and in July 1937 Rudolph moved to Winston-Salem, North Carolina. In North Carolina Rudolph began to sell doughnuts directly to retail customers, so this is often considered the chain's "birth." Rudolph apparently planned to sell doughnuts wholesale to local merchants as he had in Kentucky, but the company legend is that pedestrians caught the sweet yeast scent and asked for them directly out of the oven. Rudolph cut a hole into the wall of the shop, and this modest walk-up was the birth of Krispy Kreme's retail business. Rudolph branched off outlets into seven other cities, and in 1947 he incorporated the chain as the Krispy Kreme Doughnut Company.[114]

Doughnut chains were emerging at the same moment in the North, where doughnut shops had been settling into the cold Northeast by the 1920s. In 1925, for instance, the Boston city directory included listings for six doughnut shops, including one early two-store chain: in addition to the two Babcock Cream Doughnut and Coffee Spa shops, Bostonians could frequent Mrs. Adam's Doughnut Shop, the Johnson Brothers Doughnut and Cruller Company, the Dawn Donut Company, and Arthur J. McCauley's Cream Doughnut Company.[115] After World War II the most famous of the region's chains was established when Massachusetts entrepreneur William Rosenberg began a lunch truck business that sold sandwiches and coffee in regional factories. Rosenberg's operation began to sell doughnuts, and they soon accounted for 40 percent of the company's sales.[116] In 1950 Rosenberg opened a doughnut shop in Quincy, calling it the Open Kettle. Rosenberg drew inspiration from Quincy neighbor Howard Johnson's, the rapidly expanding roadside coffee shop that began its business in 1925.[117] Prompted by Howard Johnson's famous twenty-eight ice cream varieties, Rosenberg's company embraced what came to be called the "variety doughnut" topped with a vast range of toppings and injected with many different fillings. Rosenberg also led the way in popularizing the "sit-and-sip" doughnut shop. By Rosenberg's account, his Quincy store was the first doughnut shop to "put seats and beverages in a retail donut store so customers could eat on the premises in addition to purchasing take-out items."[118] Lunch counters, diners, and soda fountains had featured stool and chair seating for quite a long time, so Rosenberg borrowed from much of the physical organization popularized by such venues. The company soon changed its name to Dunkin' Donuts, and the chain quickly grew into surrounding New England cities. Former Rosenberg partner Harry Winokur opened the Mister Donut chain in 1955, and like Dunkin', Mister Donut would grow to be one of the nation's largest doughnut chains.[119]

Chains soon planted the doughnut flag on the West Coast. In 1940 Salt Lake City brothers Al and Bob Pelton opened Spudnuts. The brothers aspired to create a lighter doughnut and developed a mashed potato flour doughnut. The chain had about two hundred stores in thirty states by mid-1948, and while the Peltons' chain eventually disappeared there still are thirty-seven Spudnuts stores.[120] Winchell's arrived in California in 1948, and the chain counted 870 stores in 1982. LaMar's Donuts touted its handmade doughnuts first sold in a converted Kansas City gas station in 1960. In 2006 the chain had twenty-eight stores in seven states.[121] Many smaller regional chains emerged as these long-term players began their businesses. In 1938, for instance, Oram's Donuts opened in Pennsylvania, and in 1936 Shipley Do-Nuts opened in central Texas.

The most ambitious doughnut entrepreneurs began to look outside the United States by the late 1950s. In 1959, for instance, a doughnut machine manufacturer appeared at a convention in West Germany where the U.S. Department of Agriculture hoped to spur export sales to Europe.[122] The doughnut machine maker optimistically indicated that "We are going to put the doughnut on the map of Europe," though the firm soon disappeared to await better-funded chains. Doughnuts were vastly more successful in Canada, where Canadians embraced the doughnut and made it their own. Canadians were making and selling doughnuts in the 1920s under very similar conditions to those Americans faced, and scattered bakeries had relatively profitable doughnut sales through World War II. The real explosion in Canadian chain restaurants began in the mid-1950s, with mostly American firms migrating north soon after they had secured successes in the United States. These companies included the likes of Dairy Queen (which arrived in Canada in 1953), A&W (1956), and Kentucky Fried Chicken (circa 1956), all of which were among the first wave of successful American fast-food chains.[123] Few of these chains were hesitant to expand north into Canada. Dairy Queen, for instance, established its first restaurant in Illinois in 1940 and, like most early franchises, turned northward when it grew rapidly after World War II. The chain mushroomed from about one hundred stores in 1947 to more than twenty-six hundred in 1955.[124] Doughnut chains were a little slower to follow. Dunkin' was the first of the U.S. doughnut chains to arrive in Canada in 1961, touching down at the same moment as Burger Chef, just a year ahead of Mister Donut, and two years before Country Style Donuts.[125]

The preeminent Canadian doughnut chain is Tim Hortons Donuts, established by the longtime Toronto Maple Leafs defenseman in 1964. Horton and partner Ron Joyce had three stores open in 1967. Horton died in a 1974 auto accident, when the chain had just forty stores. In 1976 the company introduced its popular Timbits, bite-size doughnut holes, and the chain added a vast range of food to its menu in the 1980s ranging from muffins to soups. Hortons opened its first U.S. store in 1985 and opened its three hundredth store in 1987. In the midst of booming growth, U.S. burger chain Wendy's bought Hortons in 1995 and accelerated the chain's march into the United States just as Hortons opened its thousandth store. In 2006 there were more than twenty-six hundred Tim Hortons stores in Canada and nearly three hundred in the United States.[126]

The growth of doughnut chains was somewhat uneven between 1960 and the 1980s. By the 1970s Krispy Kreme only counted about sixty stores scattered throughout the Southeast, whereas Dunkin' had 334 stores in 1968. Dunkin' expanded rapidly throughout much of its history, while Krispy Kreme expanded much more deliberately. Beatrice Foods purchased Krispy Kreme in 1976, three years after founder Vernon Rudolph's death, and in company folklore the Beatrice management period is sometimes called the chain's "dark ages."[127] Krispy Kreme's champions criticize Beatrice's interest in expanding beyond doughnuts and departing from the chain's longtime commitment to Rudolph's original recipe. In 1982 a host of franchisees launched a leveraged buyout of Beatrice and "brought the company back to its roots" in Krispy Kreme hagiography.[128] Those roots proved to be expensive, though, and a decade of debt fanned by the buyout slowed chain expansion into the early 1990s. In the interim, Dunkin' grew rapidly and branched out into a wide range of foods, much as Tim Hortons was doing at the same moment, and Dunkin' accounted for roughly 20 percent of the nation's doughnut shops in 1986. Dunkin' expanded exponentially when it purchased Mister Donut in 1990, at that time the country's second-largest doughnut chain.[129] Krispy Kreme opened its first store outside the Southeast in 1995, when they planted a store in Indianapolis, and a year later they had a store in New York City. In 1999 the chain turned westward and opened a store in La Habra, California, outside Los Angeles. They took aim on Tim Hortons territory in 2001, opening their first store outside the United States outside Toronto. However, in comparison to industry giants Dunkin' and Tim Hortons, Krispy Kreme's 250-odd stores account for a rather modest slice of the American doughnut marketplace.

The Questions about Doughnuts

Fried dough has a place in almost every cultural cuisine, so in many ways the doughnut is perhaps Americans' creolized contribution to this millennia-old tradition. Doughnuts very quickly assumed a place at the heart of American foodways, and they found a home in a vast range of regional cuisine. The interesting thing about fried dough in general and doughnuts in particular is that their appeal can make a reasonable claim to cutting across almost every social division. Certainly few foods can claim a similar popularity. Yet this history raises a series of questions about the sort of symbolism the doughnut has assumed. For instance, exactly why did the doughnut assume such popularity? What broader cultural and social patterns drive doughnut consumption, and does the allure of doughnuts differ substantively from that of other fast foods? Exactly what sorts of identities have consumers projected onto doughnuts, and how do those identities differ from those for other foods (if they differ at all)? To understand the doughnut as something other than an abstract historical subject, we need to confront the complex cultural meanings of doughnuts.

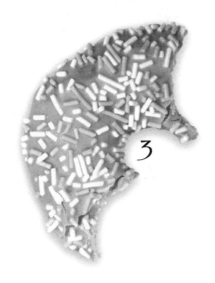

3

Selling and Consuming the Doughnut

$\mathcal{H}arrods\ bills\ itself$ as the world's premier department store, and it is difficult to challenge this somewhat audacious pronouncement. The elegant London store sells some of the world's finest merchandise under the bold motto "everything for everyone everywhere." For over 150 years the Edwardian landmark in the Knightsbridge neighborhood has sold unusual, distinctive, and costly commodities hailing from every point on the globe. Harrods may be best known for its designer goods and features like the stunning Egyptian Halls, but the most distinctive feature of the Knightsbridge store could well be its unique aroma: Harrods' attraction owes a significant debt to the alluring waves of perfume, garments, and foods that permeate the store. Harrods was born as a grocery wholesaler and tea dealer in 1849, and its renowned Food Hall still hawks an eclectic range of teas, meats, and candies whose mingled aromas fill the heart of the ground floor. Working toward the heart of the Food Hall is a delightful swim through successive waves of scent. Moving from hundreds of intermingled teas and coffees, customers pass through a powerful wall of salted meats and eggs, wade into a sweet cloud formed by every imaginable fruit and vegetable, and wind around a deep, complex cheese smell in the store's rich fromagerie. Yet the Food Hall really hits its stride when customers reach the junction of the store's candy shop and bakery, where a distinctive sweet yeast aroma emanates.

That smell familiar to many Americans comes from Krispy Kreme, which arrived in Knightsbridge in 2003. The chain's first European outlet joined a host of twenty-five fine restaurants in Harrods (at last count), and most claim a more lofty pedigree than Krispy Kreme. A Harrods guest can choose from Bretton crepes, a rich champagne-and-oyster bar, or fine Thai food, yet in the midst of such sophisticated cuisine the modest doughnut has found a very appreciative audience. Steeped in tradition, laden with bourgeois panache, and situated in one of the world's most famous shopping districts, Harrods might seem among the least-productive places for an American doughnut retailer to set up shop. In North America the humble doughnut tends to be associated with vastly less upstanding spaces than Harrods' unique food court. The world's most affluent and savvy shoppers pass through Harrods, recognizing the subtleties of countless pâtés, seizing on the latest fashion trends, and identifying the world's most attractive perfumed scents. In the midst of this show of taste and affluence we now find a crowd ravenous for sweet American doughnuts. Alongside Dior and Gucci satchels, Krispy Kreme boxes are now a fixture among passengers at the neighboring Underground stop.

The glowing public relations machines at Harrods and Krispy Kreme explain doughnuts' popularity by reference to "supply side" factors, such as store environments, brand symbolism, and the product itself. While Harrods provides an exceptionally prominent stage to hawk most any product, simply trying to sell something in Harrods does not promise it will be consumed. Before Krispy Kreme arrived, Harrods already offered a stunning selection of candies and pastries, and England was not an underserved doughnut market, either: neighborhood bakeries dot London with no shortage of breaded confections, and a foray outside the city turns up many more bakeries producing enticing pastries and doughnuts. Harrods is indeed a storied space with a rich tradition, but England is not short on such venues, and plenty of marketers besides Krispy Kreme and Harrods understand the theatrical dimension of selling goods.

Consequently, despite the clever marketing at Krispy Kreme and Harrods' rich tradition, a significant dimension of doughnuts' popularity must be in consumer demand. Doughnut sales and consumption reflect the complex intersection among marketing strategies, producers' efforts to shape consumption, and consumers' complex desires and motivations. The challenge of making sense of doughnuts or most any food is that we do not eat particularly rationally. From a purely economic perspective most shopping is rife with irrationality, since our consumption is not determined by apparently objective economic factors like product cost, convenience, healthiness, or marketing. Instead, we develop powerful allegiances to particular stores and brands; we willingly ignore the impact various products will have on our health; we are impulsively drawn to store displays and swayed by transparent advertising; we are profoundly influenced by sensory stimuli like smell, texture, and spatial aesthetics; and there is no clear distinction between the things we truly need and those we desire. Like any marketers, doughnut makers have developed a variety of strategies to reproduce our desire for doughnuts and encourage us to continue buying them, and many of these marketing strategies have been quite successful. Nevertheless, doughnuts' persistent popularity is a complex intersection of marketing, consumer identity, brand allegiance, idiosyncratic devotion to particular doughnut styles, and the complicated allure of doughnut consumption spaces. The allure of Harrods' Krispy Kreme—or any other doughnut sold in any shop—is shaped by a vast range of factors.

Eating American

When the American Center in New Dehli held an event the day after the 2004 U.S. elections, guests were feted with "an American-style breakfast of scrambled eggs, hash browns, and doughnuts."[1] For the New Dehli audience—not unlike that in Harrods—the doughnut and other American foods illuminate how those diners imagine America, so they may say more about images of America than about the objective realities of the national table. National cuisines are dynamic, ambiguous, and largely imagined sentiments about shared food and identity. At various moments and in different minds, American cuisine and doughnuts have been linked with everything from multiculturalism to patriotism to mothering, so it is a flexible albeit persistent notion. Observers who invoke national cuisines tend to evade complex trade relationships, internal social diversity, and cultural exchange across time and space. Nationalist cuisines instead paint a rather essentialist notion of what broadly defined foodways such as "Chinese," "Italian," or "American" actually imply about those nations and their subjects. The doughnut's prominence in many versions of American cuisine raises the question of exactly what doughnuts in particular and American food in general have symbolized at certain moments and in various contexts. The doughnut rears its head as symbolic of America in a vast range of contexts within the United States and throughout the world, but it ends up assuming somewhat different meanings in all those places.

Doughnuts appeared in the earliest self-consciously American cookbooks and have been couched in broadly defined nationalist symbolism as long as almost any other food, so they are often considered "American" without really scrutinizing precisely what that means. Harrods' customers likely do not really believe America is quite as fashionably retro as their local Krispy Kreme implies, and New Dehlians may suspect that their greasy morning meal is not especially authentic. When the television show *Arrested Development* featured a British-run restaurant meant to mimic American settings, it was called "Fat Ammy's" (short for "fat Americans") and served soda and baskets of doughnuts. All of these visions are distorted reflections of American cuisine and identity, yet when consumers appropriate nationalist symbolism in a commodity like a doughnut or a Big Mac they are imagining the nation, and it is worth probing what sort of America is being imagined by doughnut consumers both here and abroad.

The doughnut's heritage in the trenches has often been invoked to demonstrate doughnuts' nationalist credentials. In 1945, for instance, *How to Run a Successful Party* championed doughnuts as wartime "morale boosters." The Doughnut Corporation of America's party manual noted that in World War II "doughnuts and doughboys are buddies again, as they were in 1917. Bewildered draftees, their familiar world out of focus, take heart again when donuts and hot coffee greet them as they leave for induction. Donuts companion them from that time on." The pamphlet rhapsodized that "no other food is so heartwarming, so heartily welcomed as the donut." Yet the doughnut was cast as having equally significant impact on the home front, where "many big war plants serve workers donuts at certain hours when energy lags. . . . Workers went back to their tasks in high spirits—with renewed zest." Eating doughnuts was even advocated as a sort of patriotic duty: "Uncle Sam urges homemakers to turn to baked products and cereal foods, so that less plentiful foods can be released to help win the war."[2]

When Signe Bergman arrived at Ellis Island, the young European immigrant passed through a physical exam and "then we had some coffee and the first time I had a donut. [She laughs.] Coffee and donut and

In 1945 the Doughnut Corporation of America's endless stream of promotions included this wartime party manual, which provides numerous games that require doughnuts. (Doughnut Corporation of America, photograph courtesy of author.)

some cookies."[3] Bergman's snicker about her first doughnut reflects her awareness that something as mundane as a doughnut remains at the heart of a profoundly significant personal moment. In the first quarter of the twentieth century a surprising number of newly arrived Americans tasted their first doughnuts soon after arriving on our shores, and they often place that moment at the heart of their arrival story and American identity. Many immigrants remember their first doughnut and share Bergman's amusement at the doughnut's prominence in their memory. When newcomer Mary Dunn left Ellis Island, her family stopped in the Buffalo train station, where "we were allowed into a restaurant in that station and I can remember the first time I had a jelly donut. [She laughs]. A jelly donut and a cup of tea."[4] Like Dunn and Bergman, Josephine Jasinski also was tickled to remember that on her arrival in Chicago "I came in and the first thing I was served was coffee and donut [she laughs]."[5] To become a citizen is typically elevated to embracing the grandest ideological dimensions of nationalist identity, like democracy, freedom of religion, or capitalism, and all these newcomers likely were committed to such ideas. Yet for many of these new Americans, the contrast of such profoundly consequential citizen rights with an especially novel and innocuous commodity illuminates how such rights are invested in the most modest things.

"The Promised Land of Doughnuts": Nationalism and Doughnuts in Canada

In 2000, Krispy Kreme prepared to open its first Canadian stores in a nation already deeply committed to doughnuts and firmly attached to the country's preeminent chain, Tim Hortons. In August 2000 *Canadian Business* sarcastically dubbed Krispy Kreme's arrival the beginning of a "Holey War," calling the invasion a "honey-glazed jihad" (before 9/11 would make such a characterization problematic).[6] The magazine indicated that "Canada is the promised land of doughnuts," invoking the commonplace albeit unsubstantiated argument that "studies have shown that Canadians eat substantially more doughnuts than Americans." Yet the most substantial threat posed by Krispy Kreme was its apparent assault on national identity as it stood toe-to-toe with Tim Hortons. *Canadian Business* wondered "Why would Canadians warm up to coffee and doughnuts made by Americans? Wouldn't they feel like, well, traitors? What could turn out to be the biggest obstacle in Krispy Kreme's northern ambitions is good old Canadian chauvinism."[7]

Canadians do indeed feel considerable attachment to doughnuts, especially those marketed by Tim Hortons. One marketing journal suggested that "Coffee and donuts are to Canadians what café et croissants are to the French." Despite this suspect cultural analysis, the journal cut to the most interesting implications of Tim Hortons' capacity to link Canadian culture and doughnuts when they wondered, "The real question is: Did we get this way ourselves, or was it Tim who made us thus?"[8] Is there something in Canadian culture or perhaps even the climate that predisposes Canadians to doughnuts, or was this fervor for Tim Hortons engineered by the doughnut chain and transparently projected onto Canadian identity?

The answers to those questions are complex and involve understanding cultural and historical context, Tim Hortons' marketing, and the ways in which both become ensnared in nationalism. Steve Penfold's sophisticated study of Tim Hortons, *The Social Life of Donuts*, tackles the complicated challenge of linking nationalism and food consumption.[9] Tim Hortons was established by the Canadian hockey player in 1964, a time when, Hortons executive Ron Buist suggests, "the idea of developing a successful business solely around the sale of donuts and tea or coffee was truly unusual, particularly in Canada."[10] Yet by 2004 *Canadian Business* reported that 42 percent of its readers considered the doughnut chain the nation's "best brand," far outpacing other Canadian firms.[11] Hortons cleverly taps into powerful Canadian symbolism by embracing hockey, the country's national game, and hawking doughnuts, a food many Canadians now see as "theirs."

The notion that doughnut culture is "Canadian" constructs Canadian nationalism in contrast to American identity, or, as Penfold puts it, the Canadian "idea of America."[12] Penfold depicts a complex Canadian vision of America in which Canadians' "imagined" America marries anti-American sentiments to a somewhat contradictory fascination with and embrace of American consumer culture. This complicated local negotiation of American consumer culture has been repeated in many other countries where Americans arrive armed with commodities ranging from MTV to fast foods. The invasion of capitalism's baubles is commonly bemoaned as the death of local cultural distinctions in the overwhelming face of a distinctly American blend of capitalism and popular culture.[13] However, the Tim Hortons example shows how consumers negotiate the facile distinctions between global and local, or, in this case, American and Canadian. For Penfold, Canadians have constructed the doughnut as a sort of national "folk food" evoking a shared national community, and that nationalism has a significant impact on how Canadians see themselves. Nevertheless, doughnuts are utterly products of consumer culture, deeply shaped by American mass culture and driven by the interests of profit, even though their consumers may ostensibly see themselves resisting American capitalism or dimensions of what they see as American culture.

The Canadian mass marketing of doughnuts originated in much the same roots as American doughnut manufacturing, and the business history of Canadian doughnuts is not especially different from that in the United States. Adolph Levitt's Doughnut Corporation of America created a Canadian subsidiary in 1931 and set up a plant in 1935 called the Canadian Doughnut Company.[14] Consequently, the machines and mixes being used by the primal Canadian doughnut makers in the 1940s and 1950s were similar if not identical to those being used south of the border. Tim Hortons was founded by Canadians and can make some reasonable claim to being Canadian, but its economic and production organization was clearly modeled on American chains. Today Hortons repeatedly trumpets that it is a Canadian company, but the chain's 1995 purchase by Wendy's means it now rests at least legally in American hands. Buist admits that "Canadians devoted to Tim Hortons have worried that the chain would become Americanized," but he somewhat optimistically argues that the chain's foray into the United States means that "the Canadian chain is bringing the Canadian product and services to the United States and actually Canadianizing American coffee."[15]

Despite many historical similarities, doughnuts have come to mean something quite socially distinctive to many Canadians. Hortons' Canadian champions often take shots at American competitors. For instance, a Canadian Idol judge ridiculed Krispy Kreme's bright red light and concluded that "Krispy Kreme are the prostitutes, the hookers of doughnuts."[16] It is not clear, though, if this sense of Canada's doughnut distinction is really based on especially clear differences from American doughnut consumption. Many observers like to point out that the per capita number of doughnut shops in contemporary Canada is higher than that in the United States, which in some minds implies that "doughnut culture" must be more significant for Canadians.[17] Nevertheless, the effort to make doughnut consumption a national phenomenon distorts the complexity of consumer patterns within both countries and assumes that the density of Canadian doughnut shops signals a "doughnut culture." For instance, Buist argues that when the first Tim Hortons shop was established in Hamilton, Ontario, "there appeared to be only one other donut shop."[18] In 2006, though, the local government proudly proclaims that there is a doughnut shop for every 5,721 residents; Boston, in comparison, had a per capita rate of one store for every 5,750 residents in 2004.[19] The way various community or national doughnut proponents develop their per capita counts is a little slippery (e.g., some just count shops in the phone book), but American doughnut centers like Boston and Los Angeles clearly have high doughnut-shop densities, even alongside Canadian figures. Even then, though, it depends on what areas of those cities are being assessed. Putting aside these quantitative issues, Canadian doughnut consumption does tend to be more regionally distinct than American patterns.[20] Hamilton and Ontario can justifiably lay claim to having one of the planet's highest shop densities per capita, whereas western Canada (one of the markets Krispy Kreme targeted) is more densely settled by upscale coffeehouses.[21]

Similarly complicated American regional distinctions also tend to be distilled to easy divisions that evade various class and social patterns. One of the clearest regional distinctions in American doughnuts is drawn between North and South, but the division is typically deployed simply to distinguish Krispy Kreme from other chains. Southerners often call Krispy Kreme a regional staple on par with the likes of barbecue, and many other Americans and Krispy Kreme itself have often dubbed the chain southern. Yet, just as invoking national identity is very fluid, this southern identity can mean different things to different doughnut consumers. When the Smithsonian added a Krispy Kreme doughnut machine to its collection, the nation's attic hailed the chain as a "southern icon." When the Smithsonian calls Krispy Kreme southern, it appropriates southern identity and places it firmly within a broader American national identity. Southerners, in contrast, tend to see southern identity and Krispy Kreme in forms that distinguish both from the mainstream. Given contemporary American politics and social sentiments, perhaps no other region actually captures American social and political conservatism as clearly as the South, but southerners cling to a self-conscious sense of separation from mainstream America. Roy Blount Jr., for example, somewhat suspiciously hailed the arrival of Krispy Kreme in New York: "I have refused to harbor the suspicion that the nation's cultural capital was self-denyingly resistant to Krispy Kremes because they are (among other things constituted of dough) the diametric opposite of bagels. . . . I hope that New York's acceptance of Krispy Kreme is not ironic. Southern food in New York is often served up in quotation marks."[22] Blount cast northern culture as a polar opposite of southern culture, but in a move characteristic of southerners he simultaneously seemed to want New Yorkers to accept southern culture when they embrace Krispy Kreme. Where the Smithsonian symbolically incorporates regional cultures within the nation, some southerners see regional cuisine as a distinguishing attribute separating it within the nation. Defined this way, being southern is a complex position that revolves around the tension of seeing oneself as somehow both outside and within American society.

Canadians sometimes suggest that their doughnut shops host a distinct sort of public discourse unknown in America. Canadian doughnut-shop regular Edward Keenan rhapsodizes that doughnut shops are places to "Read, write, plot, dream, fall in love. I have done all of these things in donut shops, and encountered many people I never otherwise would have. . . . I have seen first dates and breakups, witnessed the conclusions to many drunken pub crawls, overheard conversations about politics and religion and philosophy."[23] The precise nature of this romanticized "doughnut culture" seems to vary from one observer to the next. Ron Buist, for example, does not envision doughnut shops as the philosophical spaces Keenan experiences. He instead sees doughnut shops as honest blue-collar spaces, characterizing the chain's Hamilton, Ontario, birthplace as a "good, solid working man's city."[24] However, there is no significant evidence that Canadian shops are socially and materially all that different from American shops. One Canadian unable to look past Tim Hortons' status as a business countered that "to call Tim Hortons a national institution is ludicrous. . . . I've been into dozens of Tim Hortons shops and nobody ever talks to others. All you do is line up and pull out your wallet and you pay." Keenan considers this too broad and elitist a rejection of "doughnut shop culture," but he also acknowledges that "I have yet to encounter an intellectual movement, or a widespread school of art or literature, that calls the donut shop home. . . . It seems the mythologizing of this national cultural institution has not yet begun."[25]

There is a significant amount of evidence that many Canadian and American doughnut shops alike witness profoundly important community discourse, and this may have little or nothing to do with doughnuts themselves. Given the social importance many people attach to eating together, it is reasonable that any eatery could be communally important regardless of the fare, even though some of us feel a little uncomfortable about according global monoliths like McDonald's the status of local social institutions. Canadians routinely voice the populist presumption that their doughnut shops are filled with working-class people (or at least sober middle-class folk), and this association of doughnuts and doughnut shops with hardworking people is equally common in the United States.[26] In 2005, for instance, Florida governor Jeb Bush rather ineptly attempted to build the Republican Party's reputation as populists when he wondered, "How many tax cuts have [Democrats] proposed for Joe Bag of Donuts?"[27] Bush's comment implied that doughnut consumption was the dominion of working-class folks (not affluent bourgeois), but in both the United States and Canada the claim for doughnut shops as working-class spaces stands on uneven ground at best and may simply be patently wrong. Like most chains, Hortons has always looked to expand on its consumer base. The stereotype of the shops as blue-collar magnets may appeal to many utterly bourgeois consumers and some people who really are working class, but chains have always worked to be inclusive spaces that accommodate a wide range of consumers. Hortons' initial customer base was 55 percent male and mostly working-class, but in the 1970s the chain had already begun to discuss how it could "attract more women and a greater economic cross-section."[28] Similar discussions were going on in many other chains at roughly the same moment. Penfold recognizes that what is really important is that Canadians *believe* their doughnut-shop discourse and broader "donut culture" are different; because many Canadians believe this to be the case and place this sense of their distinct national discourse at the heart of identity, whether this is true is essentially irrelevant.[29]

Other easy analyses of doughnuts' importance in Canadian culture do not hold up to close scrutiny. For instance, Penfold rejects the suggestion that Canadians' powerful connection to doughnuts is explained by the doughnut's "natural" fit with cold-weather folk. Penfold acknowledges that Tim Horton's biography captures many especially attractive Canadian qualities, since Horton seems to be universally characterized as a hardworking gentleman who played the national game and was tragically struck down at the zenith of his fame. Nevertheless, this romantic biography does not explain how the chain named for him has secured national success. For many customers today Horton himself is at best a historical figure and likely no more real than Kenny Rogers, Colonel Sanders, or Ronald McDonald. Instead, Penfold points to a tension between, on the one hand, Canadians' widespread consumption of American commodities and, on the other hand, a desire to construct an "authentic" Canadian experience distinct from American consumer culture.[30] In this case Canadians overlook the doughnut's roots in American mass culture (and Canadian chains immersed in the same socioeconomic practices) and see the doughnut's social symbolism as a product of a distinctive Canadian culture. For Penfold, Canadians' populist vision of doughnut consumption as a social leveler is a romanticized effort to construct a sort of doughnut "folk culture" despite doughnut production and doughnut consumption's concrete roots in American mass culture.[31]

Doughnuts and the American Dream

Like many other marketers, Krispy Kreme celebrates the stereotypical American dream stories that produced the chain and characterize many of their franchisees. In this sense, the nationalism Krispy Kreme celebrates revolves around entrepreneurialism and small business, which have often been the heart of Horatio Alger tales. Krispy Kreme's own history rhapsodizes that in 1937 founder Vernon Rudolph and two partners "set off in a 1936 Pontiac and arrived in Winston-Salem with $25 in cash, a few pieces of doughnut-making equipment, the secret recipe, and the name Krispy Kreme Doughnuts. They used their last $25 to rent a building. . . . With little money left to buy ingredients, Rudolph convinced a nearby grocer to lend him ingredients in return for payment once the first doughnuts were sold." When Rudolph needed to deliver his doughnuts to merchants, "he took the back seat out of the Pontiac and installed a delivery rack."[32] A Krispy Kreme fan told the *Philadelphia Daily News* that "Krispy Kreme is not just a donut, it is a culture. . . . Krispy Kreme has changed the way we do business. What an American dream! If you don't like the donuts, that is fine, but you have to love what Krispy Kreme stands for. . . . Business practicality, simplicity, and good old-fashioned common sense!"[33]

Tim Hortons also looks to the 1930s for its core values, which are not much different from those Krispy Kreme embraces. Ron Buist sees the chain's roots in "personal values that came from starting life during the Great Depression; [and] the willingness to work hard and as long as the job required."[34] Many other companies glowingly celebrate similarly stereotypical entrepreneurial origins in hardship, commitment, and good fortune, but Krispy Kreme has been especially successful spreading its company story. The stock elements of the company's originations mythology repeatedly surface in popular press accounts.[35] Rudolph himself, for instance, is routinely portrayed as having the ideal personal qualities and life challenges common to most great American entrepreneurs. In *Making Dough: The 12 Secret Ingredients of Krispy Kreme's Success*, Kirk Kazanjian and Amy Joyner paint a heroic portrait of the young Rudolph, describing him "as a good student and athlete, who always had a strong work ethic. He did chores for neighbors and helped out in his father's general store."[36] The implication seems to be that a profitable enterprise could only be originated by such a stereotypically model citizen (although American business history does not seem to universally support that conclusion).

The American dream story painted by Krispy Kreme reaches into the boardroom and extends to its franchisees. Present-day Krispy Kreme champions are eager to underscore that many of the company's administrators rose from lowly positions within the chain. Scott Livengood, for instance, grew up in North Carolina (biographies circulated by Krispy Kreme public relations always pointed out that he was raised

Much of Krispy Kreme's brand identity is based on its success evoking the firm's 1950s heritage. In 1953 this Mobile, Alabama, shop displayed many of the aesthetics that distinguish the chain's outlets today. (Photograph courtesy of Thigpen Photography.)

"eating Krispy Kreme doughnuts"). In 1977 he joined the company as a personnel trainee. Livengood eventually ascended to CEO in 1998, overseeing an enormous period of growth with the company.[37] Livengood's story was widely hailed in accounts of Krispy Kreme's success after the company was first publicly traded, but that particular American dream tale was mortally undercut when Livengood was deposed in 2005. The chain has many additional similar stories, though. Joseph McAleer, who began working for Rudolph in 1951 "as an intern making $1 an hour," eventually controlled a series of early franchises, and in 1982 he was among a circle of investors who purchased control of Krispy Kreme back from Beatrice Foods. Both of his sons became administrators in the company.[38]

The firm has cultivated the perception that securing Krispy Kreme franchise rights is a very competitive and highly selective process, so simply running a Krispy Kreme outlet is constructed as an achievement in itself. Virtually every chain preaches its exclusivity to potential franchisees, but Krispy Kreme can make a genuine claim to expanding gradually, if not choosing its partners carefully. Krispy Kreme is at the very least a smaller chain than its much bigger competitor, Dunkin' Donuts, which reflects Krispy Kreme's longtime effort to protect the novelty of the chain. Franchisees who join Krispy Kreme are typically driven and reflective entrepreneurs who can assemble roughly $2 million, leading Kazanjian and Joyner to enthuse that "It's no stretch to compare the search for a Krispy Kreme franchisee to a search for a NASA astronaut."[39] The franchisees who pilot the Krispy Kreme spacecraft include a series of prominent celebrities, including Dick Clark (who has franchises in the United Kingdom), Jimmy Buffet (Palm Beach), and Hank Aaron (Atlanta).

Doughnuts and Ambition in Cambodian America

Perhaps the most interesting contemporary American dream stories linked to doughnut marketing come from Cambodian refugees who flooded California in the 1970s. By one count in 2004, roughly 90 percent of California's independent doughnut shops are owned by Cambodians, while a more conservative 1995 count still put it at 80 percent of about two thousand California shops.[40] Cambodia secured its independence from the French in 1954 and was relatively peaceful for the subsequent fifteen years despite the nearby Vietnam War. In the 1960s only a few hundred Cambodians lived in the United States. During the Vietnam War Cambodia declared itself neutral, though the United States and South Vietnam bombed Cambodia, believing it was harboring North Vietnamese. In 1970 guerrilla Khmer Rouge forces began to gather power in Cambodia, and after five years of civil war they emerged victorious. Between 1975 and 1979, Khmer Rouge dictator Pol Pot lorded over widespread executions that claimed one to two million Cambodians from a total population of about seven million. These state-supported murders were focused on well-educated Cambodians, but famine hit farmers especially hard. A modest stream of refugees began to escape to the United States in the 1970s, and by 1980 many of these subsistence farmers joined the exodus to the United States, where most of them filled working-class jobs.

The most significant exception was in the doughnut business. When Cambodian immigrant Ken Ngak arrived in southern California he asked a fellow immigrant about the job possibilities for Cambodians: "He recommend several business, mostly doughnut business. He told me a friend of mine, who came to America when I did, live in San Jose, and now he manage a doughnut shop and own a home already. After one year in America and he bought a home?"[41] Ngak became a manager at a Winchell's, using his profits to buy an ice cream store run by his wife while he continued to run the Winchell's outlet.

There is no Cambodian pastry heritage that predisposed these immigrants to doughnuts, and in fact many Cambodian doughnut-shop owners recognize that the business is arduous and unpleasant. The picture painted by Charles Davis's 1990 documentary film *Cambodian Doughnut Dreams* stresses that doughnut-shop owners see themselves as survivors of Pol Pot, since most fled in the midst of terrorism that took many of their families' lives. Davis argues that these refugees are driven to support their own dependents after losing many of their families in Cambodia, so doughnuts simply are a convenient economic means to an end. For instance, one Los Angeles proprietor succinctly acknowledged, "I don't like anything about doughnuts but I have to do it for a living." Another lamented, "Personally I hate doughnuts. . . . [Y]ou kind of get the smell stuck to you."[42]

Hopeful Cambodian entrepreneurs seeking an economic foothold were partly attracted to the straightforward nature of doughnut production. Doughnut preparation uses premixed ingredients and some basic machinery, and establishing a shop demands relatively low initial investment. A Los Angeles area doughnut shop can typically be set up for about $40,000, which is considered an affordable initial investment for aspiring entrepreneurs.[43] An established Cambodian community provides some material support for budding entrepreneurs seeking initial loans, though the extent of such support is unclear.[44] Many

Cambodian immigrants were initially attracted to working alongside people who shared their language and culture, and the actual line of work was relatively unimportant. A California doughnut-shop manager from Cambodia confirmed that "The prospect of working without language barriers and amongst the comfort and familiarity of [our] own folk is attractive."[45] Also, the cost of running a shop can be decreased by pooling labor among close family members.

This American dream does not simply assimilate newcomers into the melting pot; in fact, one shop owner told Davis that "I always feel myself Cambodian more than American." Despite such sentiments, Cambodian doughnut-shop owners and their families have developed distinctive aspirations that are familiar yet profoundly shaped by their refugee experience. For instance, one shop owner indicated that "I like to realize my dream to become true, I want to get rid of my 84-Z [1984 Z-28 Camaro] to get a Jaguar because its my dream for a long, long time; even I was in Cambodia I think about Jaguar, that's why I jumped into the business like doughnut shop. . . . I want to enjoy myself to be happy of myself because this is my second life after the Pol Pot time so you will have, you depend on yourself you will get something in the United States it is a country of opportunity." One family member working in a Los Angeles shop remembered her father being taken away by Khmer Rouge, and in his final words to the family "he told us take care of each other . . . and he said that whatever happens all you have is your family and your brother and sisters and he said that where would we go to like get a better education because that's what's . . . going to make your life better."[46]

Cambodian doughnut entrepreneurs are still subject to the same business and personal vagaries of any enterprise, which is demonstrated by the story of refugee Ted Ngoy. Ngoy was among the earliest Cambodian doughnut-shop proprietors, and he started many subsequent newcomers in the doughnut business as well. A Chinese Cambodian who came to the United States in 1975, Ngoy found work first as a janitor and then at a gas station neighboring a busy doughnut shop. Seeing the steady traffic nextdoor, Ngoy investigated the possibility of entering the business himself. He became a manager of a Winchell's in Newport Beach and then purchased a shop called Christy's in La Habra. With the addition of new Christy's shops, Ngoy began leasing

One of the most distinctive images of a doughnut's apparent assimilative powers is this late-nineteenth-century postcard image of Mrs. Sharp Nail. Identified on the card as a Rosebud Indian, Mrs. Sharp Nail was posed with a doughnut, a significant contrast to the numerous images of American Indians in traditional garb. (Photograph courtesy of Denver Public Library, Western History Collection, X31834.)

shops to Cambodian newcomers and had become a millionaire by the mid-1980s. Ngoy held Republican fund-raisers that hosted George H. W. Bush, Ronald Reagan, and Richard Nixon at his plush Mission Viejo home. However, a passion for gambling cost Ngoy most of his fortune and his marriage. His financial collapse came just as many Cambodians were growing weary of the doughnut business and branching out into new enterprises, including liquor stores and fast food.

Cold War America, Childhood, and Doughnut Memories

Much of the doughnut's symbolism trades on its ability to evoke 1950s America. Krispy Kreme in particular has championed the notion that doughnuts evoke a cold war American heritage in which doughnuts were a symbolic glue binding families and reflecting the nation's affluence. Ageless Krispy Kreme franchisee Dick Clark makes an ideal face to root Krispy Kreme in the 1950s, and Clark himself argues that "Krispy Kreme is so popular . . . because it's a throwback to the good old days of innocence when you spoiled yourself with a treat every now and then. . . . Visiting a Krispy Kreme store . . . is a mystical and nostalgic experience."[47] Krispy Kreme administrator Jack McAleer acknowledges that the chain's success requires "capturing that time in America," an idyllic adolescence that involved doughnut consumption.[48] A San Francisco DJ likewise noted that many of his audiences spill out to Golden Gate Donuts after a show because "The fact that it's an authentic 50's shop makes the doughnuts taste even better than they are."[49]

The strategically undefined idea of doughnuts as "comfort food" recurs throughout doughnut discourse, often invoking some ambiguous doughnut nostalgia. For instance, one doughnut proponent enthusiastically noted that "Doughnuts are inherently old-fashioned, and thus great comfort foods."[50] Another observer indicated that "hot doughnuts are fast becoming the new comfort food of the decade—offering a taste of warm nostalgia in a sometimes-harsh new world."[51] To heighten nostalgia, some doughnut shops celebrate their own heritage, and almost every doughnut maker who has been in business for even a few years stresses that they use the firm's "original" recipe or an otherwise unique historical preparation. Opened in 1915, Ohlin's Bakery in

Cambridge, Massachusetts, remains in the family's control today, and in 2003 the current family baker proudly trumpeted, "We manufacture the product the same way as back then."[52]

Many doughnut marketers use their shops to evoke the past, which may mean the 1950s or may simply refer ambiguously to an earlier moment. Krispy Kreme's nostalgic air is heightened by the stylized vintage aesthetics and materials in its shops. The chain's red-and-green logo was developed in 1955 and continues to be used today in much the same form as it was first developed.[53] Four years later founder Vernon Rudolph began to standardize the stores' aesthetics, introducing a uniform green-tiled roof and long glass panels. Other doughnut shops that have escaped remodeling over the years inevitably display their age. Some stores simply manufacture this retro aesthetics in the absence of any genuine store heritage. The first Hotties Gourmet Donuts shop planned for Orlando was to be graced by a 1955 Chevy police cruiser sitting in front of a retro diner with a jukebox featuring more than two thousand songs from "the rock and roll era."[54] Tim Hortons trades on its namesake's history, but the shops are not especially retro, and many Hortons customers now know little or nothing about Tim Horton. Tim Horton's family had his pictures removed from the restaurants, but the first Tim Hortons shop in Hamilton still has a historical display that includes the store's early signs and Tim Horton memorabilia.

Retro aesthetics and ambiguous heritage heighten the doughnut's capacity to evoke childhood and family experiences. A California consumer seemed transported back to her youth when she said, "I remember clearly when I was very young biting into a warm doughnut. If there's anything better in the world than a warm doughnut, I don't know what it is."[55] One newspaper opined that the "doughnut takes us back to childhood. It's a soft, sweet, easy to eat snack."[56] Some of the most powerful doughnut symbolism revolves around peoples' similarly strong if sometimes inarticulate sentiments about doughnuts' place in their past, especially as children. This is common for many other foods that adults use to celebrate their youth. One holistic "energy specialist" recognizes that one of the ways people bond is by sharing childhood experiences, and she uses doughnuts as an example of a powerful memory. If a person hopes to create a relationship with somebody else, he or she might say "'You know days like this remind me of my childhood. . . . [M]y mother never gave me doughnuts.' . . . And we have a bonding ritual going on. 'You never got doughnuts?' 'I never got twinkies.' Bingo—friends for life."[57]

Many of our childhood memories are linked to a particular doughnut shop or one of the chains. Tennessee columnist David Spates remembered, "Growing up in Knoxville in the 1970s, some of my favorite childhood memories are of me and my sister watching the Krispy Kreme doughnuts roll off the production line."[58] Spates indicated that the "doughnut shop/factory is still there today, as is the window, and I smile every time I drive by and see little kids standing on their tiptoes to get a better look at the freshly made crullers. Nothing impresses a child like seeing an entire facility dedicated to the manufacture of doughnuts." When Krispy Kreme opened in New York, Roy Blount echoed the Tennessee columnist: "I was thinking I was 12 again, eating Krispy Kremes in Atlanta."[59] A man at a 2004 Washington Krispy Kreme opening said, "I've loved Krispy Kreme since I was [a] little boy. . . . I'll be buying these doughnuts on a regular basis."[60] A Las Vegas reporter latched onto regional identity and childhood symbolism alike when he described Krispy Kreme as a chain "long cherished by Southerners as part of their best childhood memories."[61] Such childhood attachments to particular chains can be very difficult to change as adults. One Dunkin' Donuts manager who grew up in Atlanta as a Krispy Kreme fan admitted that when he was a child, "Dunkin' was the enemy."[62]

Transparent nostalgia for mother and feminine domesticity is often associated with doughnuts and childhood memory. In 1885, the poem "Mother's Doughnuts" told the story of a young man who visited a ranch and wondered, "Wuz I Sleepin' or awake? The smell was that of doughnuts, Like my mother used ter make."[63] The smells and sounds associated with doughnuts are often evoked by scribes hoping to kindle childhood memories linked to mothering and domesticity. In the 1920s, *The House Beautiful* heralded "the epitome of domestic bliss and family welfare, frying doughnuts."[64] Juliet Corson may have sounded even more overblown in 1881 when she wondered if present-day food would ever "give half the enjoyment to my gustatory nerves . . . [as] the sight of the crisp amber doughnuts which the dear old grandmother lifted from the smoking frying-kettle to the earthen crock upon the nearest table."[65]

Salvation Army lassies routinely invoked (or were associated with) doughnuts' connection to mother. In March 1918, *Stars and Stripes* quoted a U.S. general who said the Salvation Army's "attitude toward the boys is that of a mother." The newspaper's reporter underscored this in a description of a Salvation Army camp at which the women "make cookies, doughnuts, and pies for our boys—the kind of things they liked to eat back home and that you cannot send over wrapped in packages." One of the women indicated that she and her colleagues "act toward them just like mothers. In fact, quite a few call me 'ma' and I'm proud of it."[66] Another woman agreed, telling the *New York Times* that "we thought some one ought to care for the boys as their mothers at home would do."[67]

Doughnut Marketing

In many ways the marketing of doughnuts is no different from the selling of most mass-produced goods. Doughnuts have been conventionally advertised since the 1920s. Celebrity doughnut plugs were pioneered by Adolph Levitt's Doughnut Corporation of America, which enlisted Jimmy Durante, Red Skelton, and Zero Mostel and ran television commercials that wove doughnuts into the shows' story lines. The Doughnut Corporation's "National Dunking Association" issued membership cards to its fans and included among its numbers Benny Goodman, Bob Hope, George Burns, and Gracie Allen.[68] In 1954 Elvis Presley may have become one of the doughnut's most famous celebrity advertisers when he plugged Southern Maid Doughnuts. The southern doughnut chain sponsored the *Louisiana Hayride,* the radio show that featured rockabilly artists like Elvis and Johnny Cash during their meteoric rise to national prominence. Like Elvis, Cash also did radio spots for the doughnut chain as part of their *Hayride* contract. (Eventually, Elvis was rumored to always have a box of Krispy Kremes at Graceland.)[69] *Hayride* host Frank Page remembered: "We always brought the doughnuts, hot doughnuts, out on stage and we would eat them in front of the audience and make their mouths water so, when they left, they headed immediately for Greenwood Road and the only Southern Maid Doughnut shop in town [Shreveport]."[70]

In 1919, Evangeline Booth, commander of the Salvation Army, had returned to the United States selling doughnuts for the Salvation Army Home Fund Campaign, which raised $13 million for veterans' families. (Photograph © Underwood & Underwood/CORBIS.)

Tim Hortons initially traded on its namesake's recognition and sometimes had hockey players show up at shops, but the cash-poor company had no money to launch significant advertising campaigns.[71] Hortons and many of the doughnut shops that settled on commuter routes were more dependent on the literal visibility of their shops than upon advertising, which explains the large signs gracing many 1950s and 1960s shops. Like Krispy Kreme, Hortons believed that "each customer became a messenger for Tim Hortons as he or she went out the door," hoping customers impressed by the product would spread the word.[72] Nevertheless, by the mid-1970s Hortons began producing print ads and launched television campaigns in the 1980s (they made their first television ad in 1970).[73] In the 1980s Dunkin' launched one of the most prominent advertising campaigns ever mounted by a doughnut chain when its "Fred the Baker" ads featured a weary baker being reminded that it was perpetually "time to make the doughnuts."[74]

Doughnut makers have not historically embraced advertising, though, with even the major chains sometimes eschewing most conventional mass-media advertising. Marketing of Krispy Kreme, for instance, is a low-key albeit carefully orchestrated combination of overblown fanfare and word-of-mouth supplemented by a legion of fund-raising groups hawking doughnuts to fund their bands, church groups, and various other organizations. Krispy Kreme has been remarkably successful enlisting celebrity endorsements, but these endorsements seem to come unsolicited. After Krispy Kreme arrived in New York City in 1996, Rosie O'Donnell had a doughnut conveyor belt and the chain's trademark "Hot Doughnuts Now" sign installed on her talk-show set, and she incessantly lauded the virtues of Krispy Kreme. The apartment of *Sex and the City*'s fashionista Carrie Bradshaw included a Krispy Kreme mug stuffed with hairbrushes, and gal pal Miranda had a date with an overeater at Krispy Kreme. *Seinfeld* included running gags about Yankees' owner George Steinbrenner's eating habits, including his weakness for sweets. Steinbrenner admitted, "I like doughnuts. My favorite doughnuts are the glazed from Krispy Kreme. I'm a freak for glazed doughnuts. And I like the jelly ones from Dunkin' Donuts, too."[75] LaMar's has likewise capitalized on celebrity fan Jay Leno, who declared founder Raymond LaMar the "king of donuts." The web page for Dreesen's Donuts in the Hamptons features a plug by actor Alec Baldwin and a picture of Bill Clinton in the shop armed with a doughnut and coffee.[76]

The opening of a Krispy Kreme is typically accompanied by enormous fanfare. In 2004, for instance, Krispy Kreme loyalists waited up to thirteen hours for a Washington, D.C., opening that served twelve hundred people by early afternoon.[77] The opening included a ribbon-cutting ceremony attended by the city's mayor, who proclaimed it "Krispy Kreme Day." New York governor George Pataki was unable to attend a 2001 Krispy Kreme opening on Long Island, but he did send a representative.[78] Like the Washington opening, a June 2004 opening in Boca Raton, Florida also featured prizes that included a year's supply of doughnuts.[79] One "skateboarding quartet braved afternoon downpours" and admitted that they were lured by the prospect of "Free doughnuts for a year. 'That's all we're here for.'" At a 2001 opening in Billings, Montana, Krispy Kreme set up a big-screen television in the parking lot and showed movies throughout the night to the crowd camped out for the morning debut.[80] In Lansing, Michigan, a woman and her twelve-year-old son camped out for thirteen days awaiting the opening of a Krispy Kreme, besting the unofficial record for a Krispy Kreme campout by a day.[81] Eager doughnut fans in Medford, Massachusetts, created a Web page documenting the impending arrival of a new Krispy Kreme with weekly pictures of the store's construction.[82] On opening day, a team of cheerleaders was hired to applaud doughnuts as a line slowly snaked through a merchandise tent hawking Krispy Kreme merchandise.[83]

After such lengthy waits, the moment of a store's opening is often described in somewhat hyperbolic terms. For instance, an overwrought Las Vegas newspaper reported on franchisee Lincoln Spoor's store opening on the Strip: "The doors of Lincoln's Krispy Kreme store opened and quickly became a blur of doughnuts and bodies. I saw an old man weep as he bit into a hot glazed. I saw two women embrace in delight. I heard a trucker with sugar frosting on his upper lip yell out 'Good God almighty!' I saw a woman eating a doughnut and screaming in her car, pounding her feet on the floor. I saw the fat and the thin, the old and the young, the timid and the bold."[84] Aided by such excitable reporters, these scenes are carefully orchestrated by Krispy Kreme's advance army. For instance, a line of more than one hundred people formed in a predawn snowstorm in Rochester, New York, with three television stations and one radio station broadcasting live from the scene.[85] The local media had all received ten dozen doughnuts in the morning, and their reports on traffic tie-ups came in part from a public relations firm apparently linked to Krispy Kreme. After one of these media-saturated Minneapolis openings, a local blogger complained that "Krispy Kreme apparently has quite the behemoth marketing department. . . . Talk about free advertising! What kind of kick back are the local media outlets getting for doing such a disservice to their very own local alternatives?"[86]

The company's arrival in London celebrated Krispy Kreme's and Harrods' shared embrace of the "'theatre' and magic of shopping."[87] Krispy Kreme regularly trumpets how its neon lights, formica, and retro styling make doughnut consumption at Krispy Kreme an "experience." One online fan argued that "Krispy Kreme has created an American institution out of fried flour by consistently delivering a better doughnut experience. . . . I'm not sure exactly what a doughnut experience is, but it's an American institution dammit [sic]."[88] An otherwise skeptical California reporter attending a Bay-area store opening admitted that "watching the donut-making machinery plugging away on the production floor (what Krispy Kreme calls the 'doughnut theater') while waiting in line was totally mesmerizing. The cascade of just-born Original Glazed Donuts kept on coming, bobbing briefly in the bath of hot fat before going under a thick, white, rushing curtain of glaze. The donuts emerge, shiny, with a glossy sameness. Krispy Kreme does make the prettiest donuts in the business."[89] Kazanjian and Joyner's business history of Krispy Kreme goes so far to call "a visit to Krispy Kreme a 'Disney-like' experience. . . . Visiting Krispy Kreme is an *event*."[90] That seems rather enthusiastic, but Krispy Kreme clearly understands that the heart of its "brand" has been the experience of visiting a Krispy Kreme shop. The chain celebrates the "theater" aspect of its visible production line, neon lights, green formica tables, and the bright red light indicating a batch of confections is completed. The neon light proclaims "Hot Doughnuts Now" when doughnuts are being produced in the morning and evening. Because oil tends to become heavy when the doughnut cools, doughnut makers typically advocate eating their products while warm, and Krispy Kreme cleverly turned that into part of its brand aesthetic.

Most of these changes did not occur throughout Krispy Kreme until the 1980s, when the corporation turned its attention to establishing a brand identity. At about the same time, the once-concealed kitchen was opened up so customers could see the production process through a glass wall. Krispy Kremes had long had a small window through which customers could peer into the hidden workings of the kitchen, and the chain unveiled the mystery of production as part of the experience of a Krispy Kreme visit. Doughnuts rhythmically march along on a conveyor belt, drop into hot oil, and then travel under streams of liquid sugar glazing before reaching the consumer steaming warm. If it were almost any other commodity, witnessing the production process would not likely be particularly magnetic, but at the conclusion of this process we can consume the freshly manufactured good. An otherwise skeptical *Salon* reporter conceded that there "was something implausibly satisfying about peering through the glass at the languid, inexorable progress of legions of doughnuts in their journey from extrusion to maturity. It was hypnotic."[91]

A Krispy Kreme administrator indicated in 2005 that "lately we're finding that people get a sense of comfort watching their doughnuts being made."[92] At Dreesen's Donuts in East Hampton, New York, a "donut robot" produces doughnuts in its window, and some consumers at the shop seem to derive the same sense of comfort from seeing the doughnut being made. A Dreesen's customer told a Food Network interviewer that "I like also that you can see how they're made, you can just come right up to the window and watch them being made, you know exactly what you're getting when you eat a Dreesen's Donut."[93] Doughnut machines displayed in shops like Dreesens and Krispy Kreme apparently attract some consumers with the argument that this machinery produces an absolutely uniform product, which is of course diametrically opposed to the shops which stress that their products are handmade and thus individually unique. Normally the idea of manufacturing food on a machine is not especially appetizing, but many of these doughnut machines are not particularly formidable. Dreesen's, for example, provides small doughnut machines to a string of regional retailers. The *New Haven Advocate* referred to a Dreesen machine as a "tinker toy version of kitschy Krispy Kreme's monster."[94]

By connecting with these visceral dimensions of doughnut shopping, Krispy Kreme enjoyed an especially profitable period of growth over about twenty years. However, Krispy Kreme certainly is not the only doughnut producer to understand the power of a bakery space. Top Pot Doughnut in Manhattan, for instance, also has a picture window offering a glimpse into the bakery's shiny machines and cauldrons of oil. Doughnut shops crafted to host the "sit-and-sip" customer are often enclosed in glass; New England consumers can find it quite comforting to be bathed in light within a warm doughnut shop as they peer out into a forbidding winter landscape. Almost every doughnut shop also has glass cases displaying disciplined rows of every variety, providing a pleasant contemplative hiatus between desire and consumption.

Smell may be the most powerful sensory dimension of doughnut shops. Dunkin' Donuts has long understood the power that Harrods unleashes in its Food Halls. Dunkin' focuses much of its energy on producing modest batches of high-quality coffee, filling its shops with an especially rich and distinctive caffeinated sugar scent. Dunkin' founder William Rosenberg quickly recognized that "Customers loved seeing the coffee freshly ground for each batch of coffee. . . . The smell was intoxicating. I even considered roasting coffee on the premises but that proved too complicated. All this was theater as well as quality control."[95] A New York firm that tests products marketed to youth found one teenager who advocated selling a fragrance that smelled like doughnuts: "You know when you walk into Dunkin' Donuts? How great it smells in there? I like, like, vanilla and orange and things that smell tasty. So, like, I think Dunkin' Donuts air should be, like, a smell you can wear."[96]

Doughnut shops obviously are powerful experiential spaces, and that drives much of the product's appeal. This makes Krispy Kreme's intensive post-2000 effort to sell in convenience stores and groceries particularly surprising. The chain has long promoted hot doughnuts as the heart of the Krispy Kreme "experience," but the chain expanded its sale outside its own stores and provided box directions for microwaving Krispy Kremes at home. In 2004, former Dunkin' executive Sid Feltstein observed that "Krispy Kreme's business model involves taking the product, storing and packaging it and selling it in retail outlets. The

Glazed America

doughnut isn't a very special product in that form."[97] Another observer echoed the argument that "Krispy Kreme's lost much of its cult-like mystique, based on its unique in-store experience and limited availability. . . . But that's changed due to the brand's expansion through partnerships with grocery and convenience stores." As the chain was beset by rapidly falling profits that culminated in a securities probe in 2004, stockholders even pointed to "its strategy of selling its doughnuts in supermarkets as cannibalizing its stores."[98]

Doughnut Cops

Doughnut shops were long considered dreary if not seedy spaces permeated by caffeine, sugar, and smoke and peopled by lingering night-shift workers, travelers, and cops. Because doughnut preparation typically begins very early in the morning, doughnut shops are compelled to have odd hours, and shops often have been magnets for people who keep unconventional hours. San Francisco's Golden Gate Donuts, for instance, opens at 4 a.m., greeting early risers such as "taxi drivers and factory workers." On weekends club-goers and late-night partiers empty into the shop in the wee hours, and the manager says "It gets pretty weird in here."[99]

Cops are perhaps the doughnut's most renowned consumers. The common assumption is that doughnut makers encourage police to frequent doughnut shops because they are open odd hours and susceptible to robbery, and by some accounts doughnut shops have one of the lowest robbery rates in retail.[100] One Calgary constable argued that doughnut shops are easy places to find and meet, suggesting that "sometimes the best crimes are solved at doughnut shops."[101] Yet for many observers doughnut shops evoke cops' sloth and corruption rather than their odd hours. Free doughnuts, for instance, are a fabled benefit of being a police officer, even though virtually every police department prohibits giving free food to officers. When a twenty-six-year veteran of the Anderson, Indiana, police force retired in 2004, the local paper noted that he visited Nick's Donut Shop every morning. The retiree celebrated that "I get free doughnuts and coffee for the rest of my life here. They love me."[102]

The specter of slovenly cops eating free doughnuts is often invoked to imply cops' laziness and corruption. For instance, when a New Jersey woman was asked how to cut the state's budget, she suggested that the legislature should eliminate "cops with luxury cars. There are too many of them eating doughnuts on my dime."[103] A concertgoer at Philadelphia's Live 8 was startled by the police presence at the concert, saying that the "police presence on the Parkway was amazing. You'd have sworn a new Dunkin' Donuts had opened up, the way they were all hanging around."[104] In 2005 the Middletown, Connecticut, police were accused of securing free doughnuts from the Dunkin' Donuts in neighboring Portland, where an employee confirmed that "uniformed police get served free at all of the Dunkin' Donuts in Portland."[105] This came as a shock across the county line in Middletown, where the local Dunkin' shop said that police were in fact charged for their doughnuts. Middletown's departmental cruisers were not authorized to take the trip to Portland on doughnut runs, either, leading the unhappy Middletown police representative to snap that the practice was "just unethical." Most police departments have comparable codes against consuming free food. In Sydney, Australia, a superintendent was forced to ban doughnut consumption by his officers because the local Krispy Kreme shop was providing officers with free doughnuts—a violation of force rules.[106]

Barraged by obesity stereotypes insinuating that cops are also corrupt and slovenly, some police forces have curtailed or even eliminated doughnut consumption among their numbers. Troubled by how elevated doughnut consumption apparently affected their officers' health, the Concord, New Hampshire, police department simply decreed that its officers could not frequent doughnut shops.[107] In Wells County, Indiana, the Bluffton police also willingly accepted a "No Doughnut" policy.[108] Quebec City's police department tried to create the same rule but was rebuffed by the police union.[109] Not surprisingly, cops often resist the stereotype of overweight doughnut eaters. One of the officers featured in a calendar of thirteen buff New Jersey cops acknowledged, "I want to dispel the myth that so many cops are out of shape, eat donuts and can't chase anymore."[110]

Most of the media references to cops and doughnuts are at least on their surface tongue-in-cheek. When a hapless Harrisburg, Pennsylvania, criminal stole a Krispy Kreme truck, for instance, the back door of the truck was left open, providing a "trail of doughnuts" for the local police to track. With the vehicle safely back in Krispy Kreme hands, the police representative suggested that "the manager from the Krispy Kreme might have given us a little thank you for our efforts."[111] When a writer to the *Boston Phoenix* relationship column indicated that he was smitten with a waitress at the local doughnut shop, columnist "Love-monkey" advised the writer to "walk to the counter and order a dozen Bavarian crèmes. Make sure to inform her that the doughnuts are not for you, and that you rarely eat doughnuts. This is because, for some reason, doughnut aficionados have little romantic appeal to the female of the species. That is, with one exception. . . . [Y]ou want to make sure that she isn't currently seeing a wildly jealous police officer. Since this is a doughnut shop and such establishments are known magnets for law enforcement personnel, you want to make sure about this."[112]

Officers reputedly favor Dunkin' Donuts, so when President Clin-ton's Secret Service staff met with New York City police to discuss secu-rity for an upcoming event, they brought along the president's favored Krispy Kremes.[113] A taste test conducted among Canadian police of-ficers found that they favored Krispy Kremes as well, and one officer characterized the competing Donut Time fare as "a little heavy. Not good prior to a footchase!"[114] During a 2001 Krispy Kreme opening in East Meadow, New York, a reporter rhetorically wondered why the company had placed itself on "a glum turnpike cluttered with fast-food restaurants, and around the corner from the Nassau County Jail."[115] She snidely recognized, though, that in the store's opening line, "true to an old adage, a uniformed correction officer was among the first to arrive." At least one doughnut-shop owner, though, testily refuted the stereotype that his shop was a haven for cops and launched a clumsy defense of the police. The proprietor in the college town of Kent, Ohio, indicated that "In an entire year we don't get more than four or five. The police out here do a really good job, I'll tell you that much. It's the drunken college kids. I'd want to bust some heads myself."[116]

The late-night doughnut-shop crowd clearly is not limited to cops. In many communities young people are legally barred from drinking and bars, and doughnut shops' late hours and inexpensive goods attract many of these young consumers. A blogger recalled that in her youth "the common hangouts for kids were either at Dunkin Donuts or the bowling alley. I recently traveled home for a brief visit and discovered that the spots remained the same."[117] Tim Hortons stores sprinkled throughout many Canadian communities often serve this purpose for Canadian high schoolers. Part of adolescents' attraction to Hortons and other doughnut shops is that they feature a food that is often the target of critique. A 1993 study of Canadian teens concluded that they associated "healthy" foods with parents, so eating fast food and junk food expressed generational independence.[118]

Doughnut Dives and Coffee Politics

Doughnut shops are often stereotyped as lower-class dives in which urbanites, laborers, and various underclass night owls can secure cheap, unhealthy food. In 1948, labor activist Lucy Fox Robins Lang recounted that she and fellow union members "lived on scant pennies donated by unions and other labor organizations. Many a time I lived for a whole day on a cup of coffee and a doughnut."[119] Lucille Ball reportedly lived off uneaten doughnuts in New York City diners before she secured stardom. However, today the caricature of doughnut shops as blue-collar dives is misplaced, since most of the doughnut chains and many independent shops are truly cross-class venues profoundly shaped by the homogenization typical of chain franchises.[120]

Tim Hortons' marketing director, Ron Buist, indicates that when the chain ventured into the Buffalo area in 1985 it faced "prejudice" because "The public expected a donut shop to be a shabby hangout offering poor quality products."[121] Hortons tends to trade on the image of dank doughnut shops and contrast itself to that stereotype, observing, "Others had set the pattern: dark, late-night hangouts, filled with cigarette smoke and offering stale donuts."[122] In the 1970s smoking ordinances began to remove smokers from many restaurants and doughnut shops. Some chains eager to present doughnut shops as middle-class-friendly spaces began phasing out smoking ahead of these laws, including Tim Hortons.[123] However, the picture Buist paints of the typical doughnut shop is at best a caricature that chains use to appeal to the broadest possible range of consumers. In the 1970s the chain had already begun working to expand its consumer base by moving away from the stereo-typical dank doughnut dive: "A clean store, a well lit parking lot, and clean washrooms, plus loads of fresh product in a friendly atmosphere was the perfect combination." In 2000, LaMar's Donuts undertook a renovation project intended to make its shops "warm and homey" through changes such as a gourmet coffee bar and "bistro seating."[124] The company saw the "upscale" image as an essential prelude to an-ticipated chain growth, but it clearly is also an effort to distance the doughnut shop from seedy stereotypes.

The stereotype of the seedy doughnut shop has been significantly undermined by marketers who have crafted a broadly defined bour-geois lifestyle that excludes doughnuts or significantly redefines doughnut consumer spaces.[125] The most influential of these chains is Starbucks, the Seattle-based coffee monolith whose java and pastries compete for consumers' doughnut dollars in almost every community. In roughly eighty-seven hundred stores, Starbucks' food sales focus on upscale pastries such as croissants, danishes, and muffins. Doughnuts have not made an easy symbolic fit with Starbucks and similar chains, even though the caloric counts and fat content of lattes, danishes, and doughnuts are similar. Starbucks and a series of similar chains aspire to attract an upwardly mobile, well-educated urban bourgeois, which is significantly distinct from the caricature of doughnut consumers. Much like Starbucks, for instance, Bruegger's Bagels targets an "edu-cated and affluent audience that skews female," and these consumers are supposedly characterized by "increasingly sophisticated palates."[126] Doughnuts may be absent in these menus because their blue-collar symbolism clashes with the chains' bourgeois panache. Some doughnut competitors have been more than willing to use their working-class im-age to distinguish themselves from the bourgeois Seattle chain. When Dunkin' contemplated a growth plan to challenge Starbucks' predomi-nance in coffee sales, one stock observer noted that "Dunkin' is build-ing on its red-state coffee image" (though its headquarters sits in the heart of liberal Massachusetts).[127] Dunkin' ran a 2006 advertisement campaign called "America Runs on Dunkin'" that apparently hoped to cement its identity as a "regular person's" restaurant by lampooning Starbucks' foreign drink names. As a customer stands befuddled in a store facing a series of upscale drinks, a voice-over intones, "My mouth can't form these words. My mind can't find these words. Is it French or is it Italian? Perhaps Fritalian."[128] A Dunkin' executive acknowledged that Starbucks had "popularized Italian espresso drinks. 'But we offer more of an Americanized espresso, with a more mellow blend.'" To back up their "every-person" image, Dunkin' was offering this mellow brew at prices roughly 25 percent less than Starbucks.'

The doughnut's steady popularity has moved at least some of the upscale chains to market doughnuts. In January 2005, for instance, Starbucks announced that 260 of its stores in western Washington State would begin selling Top Pot doughnuts. The coffee giant cleverly negotiated stereotypes of doughnuts as lower-class, fat-laden machine-produced products by stressing that Top Pot produced "hand-made gourmet doughnuts" from its two retail stores that enjoy a "cult-like following in the Seattle area."[129] One Starbucks critic, however, responded that "Starbucks is making a mistake carrying Top Pot donuts. If Starbucks is a true leader of Social Responsible Businesses you would not be feeding people the trans-fat laden artery clogging hydrogenated oil sponges that Top Pot calls donuts."[130]

Starbucks excels at creating store environments saturated with lush earth tones, plush carpeting, and marginally alternative music that contrast radically with the formulaic plastic interiors that characterize most chain restaurant architecture. Starbucks venues aspire to be communal spaces akin to Italian espresso bars and French cafés, and Starbucks' effort to construct its stores after these European models exploits Americans' material and social stereotypes of such venues. There may be some truth to the notion that Europeans gather in small villages and share their lives over espresso and handmade pastries, but Starbucks' outdoor seating at numerous strip malls is not an especially seamless material interpretation of those European models. However, what is more important is that many Americans immersed in mass consumer culture are attracted to the idea that a Starbucks can be a neighborhood venue despite the chain's massive size. Material changes in Starbucks stores' aesthetics and the embrace of specialized foods attempt to fulfill the European notion of an idiosyncratic community coffeehouse while ensuring that the stores are predictably profitable venues.

Like many other contemporary brand sellers, Starbucks has championed a "coffee lifestyle" that places a commodity and the chain's consumption spaces at the heart of a cohesive identity with a shared if somewhat implicit politics. Branding refers somewhat less to a particular product (e.g., coffee) than it does to a set of social values and way of life embodied in a range of goods.[131] Starbucks predictably hawks coffee, mugs, and coffee machines to extend the "Starbucks experience" to your home, but it also very profitably sells goods like CDs (e.g., Bob Dylan's *Live at the Gaslight* was sold exclusively at Starbucks) that are at best loosely linked to coffee.

Starbucks champions a range of political causes that appeal to left-leaning bourgeois consumers, such as free-trade coffee sales, sustainable agriculture, and supplier diversity.[132] This politics is considerably different from the one that the doughnut chains embrace. Krispy Kreme, for instance, is likely no more conservative than most doughnut chains and other restaurants, who are all relatively predictable champions of laissez-faire business regulation. In 2000, for instance, 71 percent of all campaign contributions from restaurants went to Republicans, and between 1990 and 2006, 72 percent of the restaurant industry's political contributions went to the GOP.[133] It is difficult to define precisely the wide range of political contributions a company can make, but by any measure most of the doughnut chains' contributions are directed to business-friendly GOP candidates and causes. In 2004, for example, one analysis indicated that 75 percent of Krispy Kreme's contributions of $97,641 went to GOP candidates; however, another observer indicated that 100 percent of both Krispy Kreme's and Dunkin's campaign contributions in the 2004 election cycle went to Republicans.[134] This led Boston journalist Derrick Z. Jackson to lament that "You probably never knew that doughnuts were a peculiarly Republican trash food." Jackson argued that the political leanings of the doughnut chains reflected "a larger war the fat pharaohs, profiting on easy-to-process sugars and starches, are waging to rearrange our brains to make us think we need the Krispy Kreme."[135]

Despite its base in historically Democratic New England, a 2005 survey found that Republican voters favor Dunkin's coffee, while Democrats prefer Starbucks.[136] Nevertheless, all the chains running the spectrum from Krispy Kreme to Starbucks laud their stores' connection to local

Pictures of soldiers and a magnetic yellow ribbon grace the wall of Long's Bakery in south Indianapolis over a cart of day-old doughnuts and alongside a warning to unruly customers. (Photograph courtesy of Wade Terrell Tharp.)

communities and skirt partisan political connections. Some chains or local franchisees have created laudable community-service programs. Tim Hortons, for instance, has sponsored the Tim Hortons Children's Foundation since 1974 and taken thousands of impoverished children to camps throughout Canada.[137] Krispy Kreme boosters Kirk Kazanjian and Amy Joyner suggest that the chain's success reflects its ethic of giving back to community through donations and fund-raising support. The chain typically devotes 2 percent of its pretax income to charities, though that figure includes doughnuts themselves and not simply cash contributions.[138] A legion of school groups, nonprofits, churches, and little leaguers have sold Krispy Kremes at a premium price for many years, a practice that one executive characterized as "more of a way to be a part of the community than to be in business."[139] However, this obscures the distinction between shrewd self-promotion and selfless community service; certainly many businesses would like to have Girl Scouts, little leaguers, and other similarly upstanding citizens promoting their product.

Most independent bakeries build contextually distinct social connections with local consumers. The Donut Wheel in Cupertino, California, is typical of the many local doughnut shops where "regulars" gather. The local newspaper heralded the shop, observing that "Neighbors have settled disputes there, students study for exams there as well as socialize, clubs meet there and the customers feel enough at home to help themselves and even do small repairs for owner Daniel Taing."[140] The eclectically decorated shop features an elk head and orange booths, and a local high school student praised this, noting that "It doesn't look corporate. It is a good place to hang out." Many of these small shops celebrate how their stores feature unique or even downwardly mobile aesthetics—"It doesn't look corporate"—to distinguish the shop from mass-market spaces like the local Dunkin' shop. Free of chain controls, modest shops can tailor their businesses to local needs. For example, when customers of Oakland doughnut shop Lee's Donuts wanted to purchase convenience-store items, owner Lawrence Khao began selling foods and even medication.[141] Jolly Chan's San Francisco restaurant China Express serves Chinese food at lunch and dinner, but in the morning it specializes in doughnuts (some customers even eat both doughnuts and Chinese food at the same time, according to Chan).[142]

While chains have a significant influence on contemporary doughnut symbolism, local doughnut shops often become distinctive reflections of their community. For instance, the crowd at the Rumor Mill Bakery in Emmett, Idaho, often included many veterans who would, in the words of one World War II veteran, "come in here, and we sit and talk. Hash over old times."[143] The bakery's owner began to hang pictures honoring these veterans, and the walls were soon plastered with over eight hundred pictures of soldiers ranging from the Civil War to the Iraq wars. The details of each Tim Hortons franchise, in contrast, are managed down to the smallest detail, just as all chains administer every aspect of their stores.

Independent doughnut shops often argue that consumers value connections between themselves and local entrepreneurs, but many chain doughnut shops have created powerful social relationships between merchant and consumer. A 2004 battle in Boston's North End, for instance, found a cadre of Dunkin' Donuts' senior citizen fans pitted against the neighborhood association, revealing divisions along generational and class lines alike.[144] The North End Senior's Club had long been eating Dunkin' Donuts at their meetings, and when the chain contemplated a move into the North End in the fall of 2004 they were warmly greeted by the community elders. However, many younger residents of the historically Italian American neighborhood resisted the new chain, arguing that it would bring increased traffic, noise, and similar disruption to the modest community. Elders argued that the resistance to Dunkin's potential disruptions was a smoke screen for class and generational bias from youthful bourgeois transplants. One senior sniffed, "All they want in the North End is high-class restaurants and condos; they're full of baloney."[145] Communities typically disagree over precisely what sort of spaces will create the most appropriate atmosphere for whatever identity they aspire to fashion. In this case, Dunkin' threatened to become an important part of the neighborhood landscape in much the same way doughnut shops have throughout New England.[146] Yet for some people, a community identity focused on eating fried flour is, charitably, undesirable.

Generations of Americans have considered local doughnut shops important social spaces. At Long's Bakery in Indianapolis, the staff has greeted customers for more than half a century. (Photograph courtesy Dennis Rinehart, Long's Bakery.)

Just as the car had provided one of the crucial growth spurts to doughnuts and fast-food venues in the second quarter of the twentieth century, from about 1980 onward auto-bound commuters again transformed the "sit-and-sip" doughnut shop. Drivers had long been frequenting doughnut shops' walk-up counters, but ever-spiraling suburban commuting propelled a dramatic increase in doughnut-shop drive-throughs in the 1980s. The transformation was especially rapid: Dunkin' Donuts opened their first drive-through in the early 1980s, but it quickly had built fourteen hundred by 2002. A contemporary Massachusetts Dunkin' franchisee concludes, "Everybody's on the go—they don't have the time to stop and park and come into the store."[147] Dunkin's embrace of drive-throughs makes more sense than that of many other doughnut shops: Dunkin' has long focused on coffee sales, which is especially well suited to drive-through delivery. One Massachusetts franchisee assessing the chain's embrace of drive-throughs confirmed that "It's not so much about doughnuts as it is about coffee."

It is unclear exactly how drive-throughs affect doughnut consumption, but they obviously bypass many of the sensory cues consumers receive in a doughnut shop. Tim Hortons added its first drive-through in the late 1980s, but the company was circumspect about not compelling consumers to come into the shop and experience the shops' distinctive bakery aroma and survey the vast range of confections laid out in brightly lit showcases.[148] Company executives were initially wary to add drive-throughs, believing that shops "would lose impulse sales. People using the drive-through window couldn't come into the store for coffee and perhaps one treat and then find themselves yielding to the temptation of a beautiful display of other products."[149] A New York newspaper warned dieters to beware of such sensory appeal in doughnut shops, which are "all about temptation. . . . Walk into a Tim Horton's, Dunkin' Donuts, or Krispy Kreme, and your senses are assailed from all directions. . . . The sharp smell of freshly ground coffee. The butter and sugar aromas of baked goods. The sight of perfectly made doughnuts, lined up attractively in their glass cases—right at eye level."[150] Yet drive-throughs appear to have had no negative impact on ledger sheets, and in 1992 Hortons opened what it called the "Double Drive Thru," from

Restaurants' competition for auto commuters is perhaps most pitched in California, promoting distinctive roadside architecture and exceptional convenience. Built in 1968, the Donut Hole in La Puente is perhaps the most convenient of all doughnut shops, and the twenty-six-foot fiberglass portal provides a unique drive-through experience. (Photograph © Ron C. Saari.)

which a shop can be accessed through either the passenger or driver's side.[151]

Drive-throughs clearly shape how chains like Dunkin' develop their wares. According to a Dunkin' administrator, "We will continue to find products that are easy to deliver through drive-thru's and easy to consume in cars. As we look at product development, we look at products that can be consumed easily with one hand so consumers don't have to drive with their knees."[152] Initially wary of drive-through marketing, Hortons now argues that its products are all mobile "finger foods" well suited to drive-through consumption.[153] The emergence of drive-through windows also has an economic impact in some communities. In some California communities, for instance, doughnuts and other foods are taxed if customers sit down to eat but not if they secure them in a drive-through. Consequently, since some portion of that tax is returned to the local government, eating in can have economic implications for small communities hungry for revenue.

Doughnut Wars

The chains often descend on communities and existing independent bakeries with great fanfare that local media invariably dub "doughnut wars." However, the chains do not universally drive out small doughnut marketers any more than Wal-Mart bulldozes every local community store. In many cases the "war" is a product of shrewd publicity by doughnut chains who encourage local media to view their arrival as potentially revolutionary. The arrival of a chain like Krispy Kreme is not necessarily bad news for independents in the same community. One Washington State doughnut-shop owner found that when a chain would open in the area "we would have a line out the door. I think it was all the hype. It's not necessarily our doughnuts. It's just doughnuts."[154] When Krispy Kreme arrived in Columbus, Georgia, unleashing competition between existing independents and the Winston-Salem behemoth, one diner proclaimed his devotion to the independent community shop: "The nice thing is they're local and they've been here for a while."[155] Demet's Donuts in Medford, Massachusetts, likewise experienced a rush of publicity following the local opening of a Krispy Kreme, leading the *Boston Globe* to conclude that if "the Southern franchise hadn't decided to set up shop . . . only Medford residents and passing truckers would ever know that inside the brick façade with the blue tiled roof, there are doughnuts of a different sort."[156] Krispy Kreme itself makes this very claim that "our competitors large and small tend to see a positive impact when we arrive in a new market."[157]

The chains also are not invariably successful after the initial fanfare dies down. Krispy Kreme opened a double drive-through in Indianapolis on May 9, 1995, the chain's first shop outside the Southeast. As he prepared for the store's grand opening, the local franchisee gushed that "I think Krispy Kreme will be the McDonald's of doughnuts."[158] Indianapolis has a pronounced sweet tooth, and the shop's location along one of the city's most prominent streets was greeted by a long line waiting for doughnuts. However, the chain closed the store in less than ten years, and an outlet on the city's north side went under while a Dunkin' shop was shuttered not far away. In 1981 Tim Hortons opened its first store outside Canada in Pompano Beach, Florida, followed two years later with a store in Deerfield Beach.[159] The chain gambled that Canadian vacationers who flock to Florida provided a local consumer base that would in turn spread the word about Hortons, but the chain was dogged by production challenges and cultural divides. Florida doughnut shops tended to close in the afternoon and were not twenty-four-hour operations like the Horton shops, and the cultural cachet the chain had throughout Canada lacked appeal in Florida. The chain eventually closed the stores in 1995, finding more successful American footholds in communities that shared more in common with Canada, such as Buffalo.

Doughnut Symbolism

In 1961, ambitious American entrepreneurs formed the Nigerian Doughnut Company to produce and market doughnuts in Nigeria. The American-owned company was reportedly making thirteen thousand doughnuts a day at the outset. Its owners were optimistic that Nigerian entrepreneurs, like their American peers, would soon purchase franchises. The *New Pittsburgh Courier* reported that the "cheery ring in the cash register is really pleasing to the doughnut businessmen. They are telling other Americans that Africa could offer a brand new and lucrative frontier for more American capital and more American enterprises." One of the attractions, they argued, was that the doughnut was "just about as American as the hotdog."[160]

The Nigerian firm folded soon afterward, but doughnuts have often played off such ambiguous symbolism very successfully. Doughnuts have been symbols of domesticity, nationalism, regionalism, and class, among other things, so the doughnut is an exceptionally malleable commodity that can be incorporated into many different consumers' foodways. The relatively low cost of materials and a shop also make doughnut shops significantly more straightforward operations than many other enterprises, so doughnuts can be sold profitably in many

4

Doughnut Morals

$\mathcal{In}$ $\mathcal{December}$ 2003, presidential candidate Joe Lieberman met with a group of New Hampshire schoolchildren to tout his "Valuing Families Agenda," which took junk food as one of its targets. Lieberman asked an assembled group of young students "Who here likes doughnuts?" and was met with what the local paper called "a resounding cheer." Lieberman sheepishly admitted, "Well, I have a confession to make. I like them too." Quickly, though, he added, "But it's important not to eat too many of them."

Lieberman is not the only doughnut consumer to feel internal tensions over his desire to eat doughnuts, although he was in a position to legislate the foods that inspired such tension. Like Lieberman, Oakland mayor Jerry Brown sought to levy a "Twinkie tax" on people who eat junk food; Massachusetts debated compelling restaurants to include at least one children's-menu item with less than twenty-two grams of fat; and in December 2006 New York City successfully banned the use of trans fats in restaurants, with Philadelphia among the other cities eyeing the same change. These and many more observers see food as a battleground that bears witness to deep-seated discord over body discipline and a variety of consumer evils that we negotiate through strategies ranging from self-discipline to state intervention.

Lieberman's uneasiness with his own food desires is commonplace among a vast range of consumers, and many of those people are willing to advocate what foods we all should eat. This is a "moral" discussion in the sense that it revolves around judgmental positions about how commodities influence character and can corrupt consumers.[1] Lieberman follows in a long line of thinkers who have felt that even rather innocuous things carry profound moral and material meaning. For instance, Alexis de Tocqueville's famous traveler's account of American life in the 1830's lamented that Americans were "restless in the midst of abundance," raising the question of whether consumers' desires were legitimate or could ever be contained.[2] Thoreau soon after launched one of the most eloquent nineteenth-century critiques of consumption, counseling Americans at the outset of *Walden* to leave the city for an uncluttered rural life.[3] At the end of the century Thorstein Veblen unleashed one of the most critical assessments of a "leisure class" that buys things simply for transparent shows of class status.[4] In all of these discussions, commodities loomed as consequential things that shape the most significant dimensions of our identities.

In a society saddled by significant public obesity dilemmas while it simultaneously champions an absurdly slender bodily ideal, the doughnut occupies a contentious landscape. Perhaps no dimension of doughnut symbolism is as hotly debated as the health implications of doughnut consumption, but the objective physical effects of eating doughnuts are really only one dimension of this discussion. Doughnuts are routinely targets for bodily discipline critiques that use bear claws as a launching point for critiques of personal character and dimensions of American society that are tenuously linked to doughnuts. Doughnuts position some consumers as willing resistors to dominant bodily disciplines championed by the state, marketers, and a host of moralists; for other consumers, though, their doughnut consumption reveals complicated internal efforts to negotiate those disciplines or reject them entirely.

Much of this discussion revolves around a newfound interest in "individual responsibility" that pins the public and personal toll of consumption on individuals themselves and not marketers, the state, or various ideologues. In present-day discussion this notion is usually wielded as an awkward cover for a variety of factions who want the state less invested in free-market consumption. In this vision of doughnut consumption, vilified foods like doughnuts have emerged as odd emblems of individual independence and personal desire. Defenders of doughnuts and various other minor vices argue that it should be outside the state's power to regulate such individual consumption by taxing goods' sale, restricting where they can be obtained, or denying them to us completely. Predictably, this perspective is well received by food producers and marketers, since they fear that public critique of their foods—or, possibly even worse, state-imposed regulation and tariffs—could dampen profits. Some observers even argue that there is not a genuine obesity crisis in the contemporary world; instead, they suggest, the attention to weight masks body prejudice, the rise of an interventionist state, and a self-interested medical establishment eager to put us all on expensive diets.

Public health advocates counter with a variety of positions that preach consumer awareness of diet's health impact. These observers do in fact make a resounding case for the underside of at least some contemporary foodways and the lifestyles that reproduce them. Some of them support rather rigorous state regulation of foodways, while others eschew legislative discipline and instead aspire to raise consumers' consciousness of foodways' impact. Many of them concede the pleasure associated with foods like doughnuts but also question whether the social links forged over doughnuts in places like school or at church mask the negative health impact of that consumption. Public health advocates are forced to acknowledge that doughnuts and many other foods are deeply embedded in American lives, so their challenge is to illuminate the effects mass-consumed foods have on collective health and probe the economic interests of mass marketers.

In the tension between such contrasting sentiments, doughnuts are among a handful of foods that have been transparently moralized as "bad" foods symptomatic of a variety of individual and social evils. Dietician Hope Warshaw, for instance, laments that there is "no redeeming quality in a doughnut. It's high in sugar, fat and calories."[5] Yet the character assessments made of doughnut consumers often reach far beyond the objective caloric content and potential weight gain harbored in a cruller. In 1988, for instance, New Jersey Devils coach Jim Schoenfeld unleashed one of the most famous criticisms of doughnut consumers following a playoff game loss to the Boston Bruins. Schoenfeld pursued referee Don Koharski at the end of the game, chasing him down a hallway and berating him for a series of calls that doomed the Devils. Koharski fell down (or was pushed, in some accounts), and he threatened that Schoenfeld would never coach again. On national TV Schoenfeld screamed his response that "You fell, you fat pig. Have another doughnut."[6] Tapping into the rich meaningfulness of doughnut symbolism and dubbing Koharski fat, Schoenfeld turned doughnut consumption into the basest of bodily and disciplinary habits.

Foodways discourses confront important public and personal health goals, but much of the popular discussion surrounding food fails to wrestle with the genuine complexity of foodways. Instead, discussion of doughnuts often paints ambiguous personal and public health interests and caricatures foods in "good" and "bad" terms that simplify complex food consumption patterns and fail to significantly change consumption or marketing patterns.

"The Morbid Dread of Fat": Doughnuts and Diet

Doughnuts occupied problematic ground as early as 1846, when William Alcott's *The Young Housekeeper* noted that pastries "whose basis is fine wheat flour, are generally objectionable. . . . Among the least objectionable—though some of these are bad enough—are, loaf cake, pound cake, gingerbread, rusks, pancakes, dough nuts, ginger nuts, tea cakes, and seed cakes."[7] Alcott's mild critique of doughnuts was part of a broad assault on refined white flours inspired by Sylvester Graham, who co-founded the American Physiological Society with Alcott in 1837. The inventor of the graham cracker, Sylvester Graham lauded vegetarian foods and whole wheat flour as part of a demanding temperance diet. His 1837 *Treatise on Bread and Bread Making* was one of the earliest assaults on refined flour, which Graham believed would ferment in the body and cause "nervous irritability." Graham proudly noted that Hippocrates himself reputedly criticized the healthiness of high-status white flour and championed stone-ground flours more than two millennia earlier. Yet Graham's fascination with digestion and flour's fiber content was no match for increasingly inexpensive refined flours that flooded the market and found their way into most breads and bakery goods.

Outside some occasional asides, there were relatively few criticisms of doughnuts in the nineteenth century. In 1864, for example, the *New York Times* ridiculed reports that lazy Confederates had successfully launched attacks on Federal troops: "Men who have just finished a feast of poultry, pie, and doughnuts are not usually in a proper condition for a 'reconnoissance' [sic] or a fight."[8] Yet a few observers began to ridicule doughnuts and establish them as a food to criticize sarcastically. When Julian Ralph visited Holland in 1899, for instance, he recognized the Dutch origins of the American doughnut. However, he questioned the effect the fried pastry had on American stomachs, joking that the doughnut had arrived in "our newborn nation to fasten its dyspeptic clutch upon our people."[9]

Similar lamentations that doughnuts induced indigestion and slovenliness were at best sporadic, and into the early twentieth century there were no consistent critiques of obesity, much less of specific foods that fattened their consumers. For instance, an 1880 *New York Times* article argued that "the morbid dread of fat which has in recent years become fashionable has no foundation in physiological fact. . . . It is not true that special forms of food determine fat."[10] This position would rapidly become untenable, but relatively few nineteenth-century analyses linked doughnut consumption to a sustained critique of American foodways.

In 1907 Yale nutritionist Russell Chittenden was among the physicians and scientifically armed commentators who believed Americans "eat too much," and Chittenden charged that American foodways explained swelling obesity and health problems.[11] This increased interest in diet and a less-ample bodily ideal would not seem to be an especially good moment for doughnuts' 1920s mass popularity. The doughnut's ascent in the 1920s makes perfect sense given increasingly mobile urban communities, increasing consumer prosperity, and the rise of mass-produced doughnuts, but in relation to period bodily discipline ideals this ascent is somewhat oddly timed. In the 1920s the once-ample ideal female form had given way to a tall, gaunt bodily ideal, a vision of femininity personified by flappers. Some of the 1920s taste for slender bodies was simply a matter of accommodating rail-thin flapper fashions, but nutritionists had begun to voice concerns about the relationship between foodways and health problems that favored this slender female form.

Dietary balance quickly became a target for crusading nutritionists. In 1929 an analysis of the nutritional qualities of children's breakfasts concluded that few pupils ate healthily at home and that there was "a definite need for education as to what constituted a breakfast." The report lamented that "children seldom eat more than a doughnut, or a piece of cake and a cup of coffee."[12] A host of food producers attempted to capture Americans' newfound interest in diet and nutrition by touting their products' healthiness. In some cases this was inspired by attacks on the product. White bread and flour, for instance, came under renewed fire, inspiring the likes of General Mills' Betty Crocker to tout white bread as a nutritious diet food.[13] Betty Crocker, of course, was not a real person, but in a clever piece of advertising and promotion she would become more trusted than most dieticians.

Doughnut advocates, though, may have outdone General Mills in securing a hired expert for the cause. The Doughnut Corporation of America enlisted surgeon J. Howard Crum, whose 1941 book *Beauty and Health: A Course in Loveliness* outlined a women's beauty program that provided diet tips, hints on personal appearance, and a primer on plastic surgery.[14] But the most interesting detail of Crum's book was his improbable "doughnut diet." In 1941 Crum appeared at New York's International Beauty Show among thirty thousand American beauty-shop owners to evangelize for his unusual diet. The *New York Times* was justifiably amused that "Attention has been centered on the 'donut diet' developed by Dr. J. Howard Crum, whose idea of dunking away pounds should prove palatable and nourishing to the overweight woman who wants to reduce without self-denial."[15] Crum advocated what he called a "mono-diet, or a menu consisting largely of a single item of food," and he provided a choice between either shredded wheat or doughnuts. Given the rather dreary possibility of steady consumption of shredded wheat, the doughnut option clearly attracted more attention at the beauty show and in the press. Crum professed to be drawn to the doughnut because he was seeking "a nutritious healthful food that not only would be enjoyed and relished by most people, but also could be secured in any part of the country at a minimum cost."[16]

Crum recognized that "some people may raise their eyebrows and smile when the idea is first suggested to them," and the idea of eating eight doughnuts a day to lose weight certainly did sound suspect to many observers.[17] Much of the doughnut defense launched by shills like Crum attempted to refute the notion that doughnuts were "indigestible" and lacked nutrition. By World War II the explosion of doughnut shops had unleashed a variety of unpleasant doughnuts on consumers, and there was a somewhat well-deserved reputation for homemade doughnuts also being of uneven quality. However, the Doughnut Corporation of America argued that machine-produced doughnuts and standardized supplies—both of which they supplied to an increasingly large number of doughnut shops—could eliminate unsavory doughnuts. A 1944 Doughnut Corporation pamphlet proclaimed that "modern tested quality doughnuts are *surface-fried,* and the temperature is carefully controlled. No fat-soaked donuts today! Just light, fluffy, golden-brown cakes, easily digested, quickly absorbed, and used by the body to a far greater degree than many other foods." In the midst of wartime clamor for vitamin-enhanced foods, Crum argued that machine-produced doughnuts' added nutrients and standardized production made them superior to homemade competitors and the doughnuts hand-fashioned in many shops. He admitted that some "people have the idea that the doughnut is a very indigestible article of food. No doubt that this is true in the case of some doughnuts, and I am frank to say that too often the homemade variety is indigestible. But after experimenting with other foods with rather indifferent results, I finally became acquainted with the machine-made doughnut purchasable in any food store today."[18] Crum's support for machine-made doughnuts is not surprising: he appeared in promotional literature for the Doughnut Corporation of America, which happily distributed copies of his diet.

Facing a public interested in nutrition, food manufacturers marshaled a host of suspect scholarly studies supporting their claims to nutrition. Crum followed suit by hailing "a report from the Department of Physiological Chemistry of Yale University stating that they have made very extensive tests on the digestibility of machine-made doughnuts and have determined beyond question that their digestibility is equal in every way to bread and butter." The tenor of Crum's defense reflects that manufacturers were keen to portray doughnuts as healthy, and manufacturers heralded a host of newly improved doughnuts. For instance, a 1941 *Nation's Business* article indicated that "recently doughnut mixes with vitamins added have been introduced to keep pace with the general vitamin 'movement' throughout the country and to make the doughnut still more important as a food. Elaborate tests have been conducted to demonstrate the nutritious qualities of the doughnut and further proofs of its digestibility have been offered to medical and other agencies seeking such information."[19] This notion of adding vitamins to foods gained significant momentum during World War II. In 1941, for example, the Millers National Federation announced they were preparing to unveil a "superflour" enriched with vitamins that were escaping wartime consumers.[20] However, the government denied the Doughnut Corporation of America the right to hawk "Vitamin Donuts" or their alternative term "Enriched Donuts" and required them to use the term "Enriched Flour Donuts."[21]

The search for a healthy doughnut was not quickly abandoned. In September 1954 the persistent Doughnut Corporation of America prepared for its annual celebration of National Donut Month with a promotion for yet another nutritious doughnut. The latest pastry was referred to as the "Cornell-recipe" doughnut, devised by Cornell University and the New York State Department of Mental Hygiene as "a nutritious doughnut for its hospitals." The doughnut's inventors trumpeted that it was "24 per cent higher in protein than standard doughnuts, 26 per cent higher in calcium and 30 per cent higher in phosphorous and iron. They have three times as much thiamine as the regular product, two and a half times as much riboflavin and twice as much niacin." Their inventors declared that the doughnuts would provide "those who breakfast solely on coffee and 'sinkers' a way to bolster that meal nutritionally. They are a sound snack provided one's waistline is not of such proportions that anything between meals is forbidden."[22]

In the 1950s the Doughnut Corporation of America joined forces with the American Dairy Association, hoping to capitalize on government support for dairy consumption and bask in milk's symbolism as a healthy food. Milk had been consumed with doughnuts from early in the century, especially as each became defined as a breakfast food. When Christine Sorensen arrived at Ellis Island and received her first food on American soil, a volunteer "gave every person a glass of milk. And then the other girl came following behind and she handed everybody a doughnut. . . . [T]he only thing I can remember is the milk and doughnuts. I have never forgotten that."[23]

Milk marketing provided a solid model for doughnut producers aspiring to sell ever-more doughnuts. Milk producers aggressively promoted their product beginning in the 1920s, but because of milk's expense few Americans actually drank the prodigious quantities recommended by nutritionists from World War I onward.[24] In 1927 an American Public Health Association committee pronounced that there was "direct and convincing evidence that milk is a necessity for children, averaging a quart a day."[25] Adults were expected to consume a pint a day, but milk was costly and few interwar Americans were actually drinking anything close to the proscribed levels.[26]

Milk producers met this challenge by launching a series of advertising campaigns lauding milk's health benefits. By 1934 the American Dairy Science Association was meeting in Utica, New York, with marketing of milk at the top of its agenda.[27] Four years later a coalition of dairy organizations met to formulate a national advertising campaign. The meeting was driven largely by excess butter production, but the dairy producers claimed as their primary goal "an aggressive campaign to acquaint consumers with the nutritional and appetizing features of dairy products."[28] The American Dairy Association was formed in 1939 and became the voice of milk producers during and after World War II. Despite the war, the Dairy Association spearheaded an expensive campaign beginning in 1940, and the government encouraged Americans to continue consuming milk during World War II.[29] A 1941 George Gallup poll indicated that half of all American families still consumed less than half of the recommended amounts, but Gallup also found that two-thirds of Americans at least knew that a quart of milk a day was recommended.[30] After the war the American Dairy Association partnered with doughnut producers in one of the dairy association's many cold war campaigns.[31] In 1953 a brochure for grocers selling doughnuts and milk suggested that the two products were exceptionally high-volume goods, arguing that "the average doughnut customer buys 50 packages of donuts a year. The average milk customer buys 150 quarts a year."[32] The manufacturers encouraged retailers to place doughnuts near the dairy case to encourage impulse purchases, which by their analysis accounted for 85 percent of all doughnut sales.

Dieting, Carbohydrates, and Doughnuts

The dieting impulse remained remarkably resilient into the 1960s, and in 1960 one New York fashion designer suggested that women were becoming "figure-conscious . . . for reasons of health, youthfulness, and overall appearance."[33] A flurry of mass-produced low-calorie and diet products emerged in the 1960s to feed such sentiments. In December 1960 the *New York Times* was skeptical of the flood of fad diets circulating in Gotham but admitted that "the public preoccupation with dietary problems seems here to stay."[34] Food producers contemplating their profit margins recognized the depth of commitment to dieting and began producing a vast range of diet foods. According to one straight-talking manufacturer, the underlying motivation was that "there's money in it."[35] There is no especially persuasive evidence for a sea change in foodways, as most 1960s groceries included a vast range of diet foods sharing shelf space with profoundly unhealthy foods. The marketplace seemed able to accommodate both doughnuts and their newly arrived low-calorie kin such as Sweet'N Low and Tab, and in many ways the grocery counter harbors a similar schizophrenia today.

Few diet programs have been as closely linked to doughnuts as "low-carb" diets. Low-carbohydrate consumption diets were first described by William Banting in his 1864 study *Letter on Corpulence*. Various low-carbohydrate plans have since appeared under names such as the "DuPont diet" (some DuPont executives supposedly were put on it in 1953, which DuPont denied); the "Air Force Diet" (1960, though like DuPont the Air Force claimed no connection to it); the "Calories Don't Count" diet (1961, which discouraged exercise); and even the "Drinking Man's Diet" (a 1964 version that featured combinations like martinis and filet mignon).[36] These carbohydrate-restricted diets did not meet with universal support from physicians. In 1965 Harvard physician Jean Mayer unloaded on low-carbohydrate diets, saying that he considered them "equivalent to mass murder."[37]

Such pronouncements, though, certainly did not sound the death knell for low-carbohydrate diets. The most popular of these came when New York cardiologist Robert Atkins published his low-carbohydrate diet in *Harper's Bazaar* in 1966. Atkins followed it with a book-length version called *Dr. Atkins' Diet Revolution* in 1972, and in 1992 the Atkins diet resurfaced to mass popularity and spawned a host of new low-carb plans. In early 2004, though, there was relatively little complaint coming from doughnut makers, and in February one newspaper even noted that "Despite the Atkins, the South Beach and the Lindora diets,

America's new favorite treat is the fried, yeast-risen doughnut."[38] The various low-carb diets borrowing from Atkins's formulation targeted their wrath on everything from bagels to Wonder Bread, but doughnuts were rarely if ever singled out as special offenders. Yet as low-carb diets won increasingly more media attention, nervous marketers attempted to find ways to accommodate the diets, which was a significant challenge to bakers and doughnut producers.

The most significant salvo from doughnut producers came in 2004 when Krispy Kreme very publicly blamed low-carb diets for the company's rapidly collapsing earnings. CEO Scott Livengood professed in a May 13, 2004, CBS story that "until recently, the low-carb trend had 'little discernible effect on our business.' Now, he said, 'It's impossible to predict if low-carb is a passing fad or will have a lasting impact.'"[39] Livengood was concerned that "recent market data suggests consumer interest (in low-carb diets) has heightened significantly following the beginning of the year and has accelerated in the last two to three months."[40] In a shareholder meeting he was even more pessimistic, believing that low-carb "diets leaving little room for deep-fried treats will remain popular for a long time." Livengood lamented that "In 30 years in this business, I've never seen anything that rivals what has occurred over the last three months."[41]

It is unclear exactly what happened in the period between February and May 2004 that made low-carbohydrate diets such a threat, because the threat was apparently not hitting the competition. Dunkin' Donuts, for instance, indicated that it had not registered any significant effect on sales as a result of low-carb diets. Dunkin' released a statement that "We are paying attention to consumers' increased interest in low-carb foods. However, we have not seen any recent decline in our baked goods sales of which doughnuts are a major contributor. In fact, in each of the past 12 weeks we have exceeded our overall sales goals for the business."[42] While parent corporation Wendy's experimented with low-carb combo meals, Tim Hortons reported in April 2004 that same-store sales rose 12.4 percent at its American franchises and 9 percent in its Canadian stores.[43] LaMar's Donuts introduced a square low-carb doughnut in November 2004 called the "Fifteener" (containing fifteen grams of carbohydrates), whose shape ostensibly distinguished it from their normal doughnuts. However, in the first half of 2004, LaMar's reported a sales increase of 15 percent over the previous year, so the chain likely was simply attempting to boost sales by diversifying its line.[44]

LaMar's profit increase may reflect the increase in its doughnut prices, but the picture of industry healthiness in the face of low-carb diets clearly does not support Krispy Kreme's analysis of low-carb's impact on sales. Low-carb diets received extensive media coverage, and at least a few observers echoed Livengood's dire predictions or assumed low-carb diets' conquest. A *Philadelphia Daily News* reporter concluded hopefully, "I like to think some people may be choosing to eat oatmeal and bananas and skim milk for breakfast instead of donuts, good carbs instead of empty, sugary, high fat treats. While this trend isn't good for Krispy Kreme, it's gotta be good for the nation's health."[45] One reader responded that "As a die hard Krispy Kreme fan, who has been weight conscience [*sic*] and in pretty good shape, I must say that everything is good in moderation." Yet many observers appear to have overestimated the power of low-carb diets or underestimated the allure of doughnuts. J. Scott Wilson, for instance, wrote in his May 2004 online chronicle that "doughnuts are probably the one food on earth most vulnerable to the low-carb mania currently gripping America by its wallets and wattles. As the most decadent of doughnut creations, Krispy Kreme, is taking it on the chin as more and more of my fellow chubsters fall into the Atkins or South Beach lockstep."[46]

There is not especially good evidence that low-carb diets had a significant negative impact on doughnut sales. Some of this may reflect long-term resistance to the contorted effort to produce healthy doughnuts. A 2003 report noted that when Dunkin' had tested "better-for-you doughnuts, they flop. An oat-bran doughnut in the '80s was a bust. And whole-wheat doughnuts sell so-so."[47] Most measures of industry growth suggest that doughnut sales remained brisk throughout the ascent of low-carb diets. One industry study on the growth of doughnut restaurants in 2004 indicated that their sales had increased 9.2 percent over 2003, outpacing the overall restaurant-industry average of 7.2 percent growth.[48] Sales in the bakery/café trade in 2004 grew 22 percent over the previous year, which also undercuts claims that low-carb diets were gutting doughnut and bakery sales. One prescient trade magazine rejected the argument that low-carb diets had a significant impact on doughnut sales, suggesting that "donuts continue to represent fun, a treat, and a personal indulgence that will continue to outweigh concerns about health and expanding waistlines for many years to come."[49]

Nevertheless, Krispy Kreme announced it was designing sugar-free doughnuts to accommodate low-carbohydrate diets, and a host of other doughnut producers and fast-food chains began considering if not developing similar products. Bake'n Joy Foods of North Andover, Massachusetts, for example, produced the CarbSubtract muffin for sale in the bakeries and stores it supplied throughout the Northeast, and neighbor Joseph's Middle East Bakery concocted a low-carb pita bread and tortilla even though the owner griped that "It's outta control, the low-carb thing."[50] The owner of Heav'nly Donuts in nearby Metheun complained that he had no success selling low-carb muffins and had seen no impact of low-carb diets on his sales. Still, he admitted, "All my trade magazines, it's low-carb, low-carb, low-carb. It hasn't really affected me in a negative way, so I'm going to stick with what we're doing."[51]

Some Krispy Kreme investors suspected that the company was using Atkins as a desperate smoke screen for internal management problems, including rapid expansion. One stock analyst admitted that low-carb diets had not helped Krispy Kreme, but he pointed to rapid store expansion and low profits in new stores as equally significant factors in the chain's problems.[52] Eventually it was a stockholder lawsuit alleging misreported sales that sent the company's stock tumbling, not the onslaught of low-carb diets. While Krispy Kreme lamented the impact of these diets, many dieters migrated away from the low-carb plans. In 2004, 9.1 percent of Americans were on some version of a low-carbohydrate diet, but in 2005 only 2.2 percent of Americans made the same claim.[53] A 2004 study noted that 17 percent of American households had a member who was on a low-carb diet, but 19 percent included a member who had abandoned a low-carbohydrate plan.[54]

At least some diet defenders had the doughnut in their sights as a particularly problematic low-carbohydrate food. In 2005, for instance, low-carb proponent Jimmy Moore declared that "there is one food that you should absolutely avoid completely when you are on a low-carb lifestyle (or ANY weight loss plan for that matter!). The worst possible food you could eat when you are livin' la vida low-carb is a doughnut."

Moore clearly recognized the calorie- and carbohydrate-dense under-side of doughnuts, but at the same time he admitted that "Not only are they chock full of sugar and white flour, but they can be extremely addictive, too. Have you tried just eating one of these, especially when they are hot and fresh? Impossible! As the top baked dessert in America today, it's hard to avoid this innocent-looking food that can literally destroy your low-carb progress. With doughnut shops on nearly every corner, these little morsels of carbiliciousness show up in all sorts of places—the office, at church, at parties and even in your own home!"[55] The challenge doughnuts posed was not simply in their carbohydrate assault; instead, they were woven into the fabric of everyday life and individual desire in ways that made them especially difficult to resist (at least for Moore). Such defenses of low-carbohydrate diets, though, were beginning to subside in 2005, and once-prosperous producers selling low-carb meals suffered as weary dieters wandered away from their plans. Atkins Nutritionals, which bore the name of low-carb guru George Atkins and sold low-carbohydrate foods conforming to his plan, filed for bankruptcy in 2005.[56]

Health Discourses and Bagels

In the 1980s doughnuts were faced by competing marketers who seized on the doughnut's reputation as an unhealthy food. The primary chal-lenge came from bagels, which are routinely touted as being a healthy alternative to doughnuts while playing off their bourgeois intelligentsia symbolism. Polish food regulations first mention hard-glazed, boiled rolls referred to as *beygls* in 1610.[57] The rolls were initially created to be given to new mothers, and eastern European immigrants eventually brought bagels with them to the United States in the late nineteenth century. A scatter of small bakeries produced them through the early twentieth century, but they primarily attracted Jewish consumers and had no significant role in mass foodways.[58]

The foundations for the bagel's transition from ethnic staple to mass-produced food began to be laid in the second quarter of the twentieth century, though the bagel did not become a mass-consumed food as rapidly as doughnuts. In 1927 one of the most famous bagel makers,

Lender's Bagel Bakery, was founded by Polish baker Harry Lender.[59] Lender had recently arrived in West Haven, Connecticut, and was apparently the first marketer to produce the rolls outside New York City.[60] Yet while the doughnut was becoming a common mass-produced food, Lender's bakery sold hand-rolled bagels to its mostly European neighbors for another thirty-five years without expanding significantly.

Bagels remained a specialized northeastern food made by Jewish bakers and eaten primarily by Jewish consumers, and much of this reflects its distinctive production tradition. Doughnuts became mass-produced, machine-made goods with little or no conversation, but bagels were firmly rooted in a handcrafted tradition controlled by unionized bagel makers. While doughnuts poured out of doughnut machines in numerous small shops administered by semiskilled laborers, bagel producers resisted relinquishing control of bagel production to aspiring mass marketers. Bagels remained a handcrafted staple in many New York bakeries through the 1950s, but there were constant tensions between bagel makers and manufacturers who wanted to produce bagels outside union control and handcrafted conventions. These disputes resulted in a series of union strikes that recurrently cut off the bagel supply in the first two decades after World War II.[61] After one strike was resolved, the *New York Times* was relieved to note that bagels' "return comes just in time for restoration of an old New York Sunday morning tradition: bagels, cream cheese and lox."[62] In 1960 bagels were still a specialty food that the *New York Times* noted "are often compared with doughnuts, although in terms that are not exactly complimentary. Sometimes bagels are called varnished doughnuts. They also are known as doughnuts with rigor mortis."[63] Yet that same year, culinary observers Beatrice and Ira Henry Freeman surveyed New York's thirty bagel bakeries producing 250,000 bagels a day and concluded that "since World War II, the Gentiles have all become converts to bagels."[64]

The bagel union's iron grip on salaries and working conditions and its commitment to handmade bagels did not make bagels an easy candidate for the sort of franchising and mass production common to doughnuts by the 1960s. In 1954 Harry Lender had already installed a walk-in freezer to preserve freshly made bagels prior to delivery, and by the late 1950s his son Murray led the charge to sell them on a wider scale and pre-slice the bagels, which made them toaster-friendly.[65] In 1962 the Lenders developed machines that could produce roughly three hundred dozen bagels an hour, began steaming the bagels rather than boiling them (to cut down production time), and moved their production outside the Northeast.[66] The Lender's operation looked toward the national marketplace, rejecting established bagel-making traditions and focusing on how it could make bagels a mass-consumed food. Frozen bags of Lender's bagels soon began appearing in supermarkets throughout the country, and they were made in a size that could be easily prepared in a standard toaster. In 1965 Lender's launched an advertising campaign that moved the *New York Times* to announce, "Pumpernickel people and doughnut-dunkers are being urged to unite—behind a rolling bagel juggernaut."[67] Lender's ads recognized the bagel as an "ethnic food," just as pizza had been before its ascent to mass foodways, and Lender's aspired to expand its consumer base and secure "the national status of pizza within four years." In 1977 Lender's sold 180 million individual bagels, accounting for $10 million in revenue.[68]

The real ascent of bagels came in the 1980s and 1990s, when they left grocery store freezers and appeared in chains throughout the country. There had been significant changes in bagel manufacturing and marketing by the early 1980s. The Lender family, for instance, sold their bakery to Kraft in 1984, and Kraft lauded the delectable combination of its Philadelphia Cream Cheese with bagels.[69] New flours and the addition of sugar and flavorings turned the once-staid and hard Jewish bagel into a soft roll that came in numerous designer flavors. This new, Americanized bagel found a home in some doughnut shops, and chains specializing in bagels gained their first substantial foothold. Long dedicated to a blue-collar image not normally associated with bagels, even Dunkin' Donuts responded to the rise of bagels by peddling its own and becoming the nation's biggest bagel seller in the mid-1990s.[70]

By the early 1990s some observers believed that the doughnut's popularity had been overtaken by the bagel.[71] In 1989 bagels accounted for 3.5 percent of breakfast food sales, but this figure had soared to 12.8 percent in 1998.[72] Bagels had by that point secured a somewhat undeserved claim to healthiness, and it was a claim sometimes staked in diametric opposition to doughnuts. When a Tufts University team quizzed

Dunkin' consumers on whether a bagel with cream cheese or a chocolate doughnut was more healthy, virtually every consumer considered the bagel the healthy alternative.[73] Yet bagels are almost always much larger than doughnuts, and even a modest cream cheese deposit adds up to 550 calories and 13.5 grams of saturated fat (the recommended daily allowances are now 2000 calories and 25 grams of saturated fat). In comparison, a yeast doughnut typically packs between 170 and 270 calories and about six grams of saturated fat, and a cake doughnut carries a punch of 290 to 360 calories and twelve grams of saturated fat.[74] One Buffalo doughnut consumer taken in by the bagel's reputation admitted that "My goal today was, I was going to come in for the 12-grain bagel. . . . But then I thought, well, it's too early to have the really good stuff—so I'll get the doughnuts."[75]

At century's end, though, the doughnut appeared to have weathered the storm, with bagels' popularity decreasing from 12.8 percent of breakfast food sales in 1998 to 9.3 percent in 2004.[76] William Safire believes the doughnut's resurrection in the face of the bagel's challenge reflects a significant shift in national sentiments. Safire cleverly implies that the doughnut's appeal hinges on its openly unhealthy yet comforting nature. "The guiltily gulped doughnut has held fast to its liberal essence," he argues. "Despised by dieters, it remains deliciously feminine, sinfully sweet and outrageously hedonistic. No wonder the doughnut—like excesses in art and hypersensitivity in sexual relations—is staging a comeback. . . . Today's doughnut knows what it is and defiantly asserts its fattening identity."[77] Put this way, doughnut consumption looms as a personal excess that consumers embrace, and we would expect such willingly accepted excess to flourish in the historical moments when we embrace desire. Safire clearly recognizes that doughnuts thrive in a culture of desire that eroticizes longed-for things like doughnuts and shuns deferred gratification. This somewhat heroically casts doughnuts as reflections of our honest desire (or perhaps our unbridled hedonism), though it does not promote much critical reflection on doughnuts' long-term health effects. If Safire is correct, consumers perhaps circumspectly accept the doughnut's potential impact on their waistlines, but they evade the most troubling dimensions of this and instead embrace their desire for doughnuts.

The eroticization of doughnuts is cleverly captured by this "Christy Creams" costume. With the promise that "This Little Sweetie will serve up your goodies hot, fresh and cream filled," the costume highlights the profound desires often associated with pastry consumption. (Photograph courtesy of Dreamgirl International.)

Doughnuts in the Fattest Cities

William Safire's fierce defense of doughnuts is in distinct contrast to a doughnut assault that has come from numerous quarters. In 2001, for instance, *Men's Fitness* began to inventory America's "fattest cities" on a yearly basis, and doughnuts became one of the factors it used to evaluate cities' claim to fatness. In the magazine's parlance, ranked cities fall into either "fat" or "fit" categories. This superficial polarization certainly clouds the complexity of public health issues, but it is a familiar and acceptable dualism to many exercise junkies and couch potatoes alike. The magazine uses a complicated litany of data to measure a community's overall healthiness, including gyms per capita, frequency of fruit and vegetable consumption, percentage of obese or overweight residents, air quality, and average time spent watching television. Another factor used to measure a city's healthiness was the number of doughnut shops per capita, a familiar but mostly emotional appeal equating doughnut consumption with a communal absence of body discipline.

The linkage between doughnuts and body discipline is certainly not without support. When the Physicians Committee for Responsible Medicine lamented the state of unhealthy airport food, they too used doughnut shops to illuminate offenders. Their report complained that John F. Kennedy International in New York, for example, "plays host to several McDonald's, Krispy Kreme Doughnuts outlets, and even a kosher deli that does not offer a low-fat, high-fiber option."[78] Many of the nation's "fattest" cities in the *Men's Fitness* assessments seem to share an attraction to doughnuts. In 2005 the nation's "fattest city," Houston, boasted more than twice the national average of doughnut shops per capita; runner-up Philadelphia had nearly triple the national average; and sixth-"fattest" city Dallas had the nation's third-highest doughnut shop per capita ranking.[79] (In the *Men's Fitness* survey the country's leading offender in doughnut shops per capita was Fort Worth, Texas, which found itself at fourteenth in the overall 2005 national rankings).[80]

The politics of denigrating whole communities by branding them "fat" is at the very least complicated, and in this case the messenger's concern for public health is questionable. *Men's Fitness* touts its target reader as a "sophisticated man," and its pages revolve around a lifestyle of ripped abs and masculine beauty. Within the pages of *Men's Fitness* these attributes are secured through nutritional discipline and exercise regimes, consumption (e.g., fashion), and heterosexuality. The genuineness of the magazine's interest in transforming community health is somewhat suspect, and the socially loaded designation as a "fat city" certainly sparks a considerable amount of public discussion. When Detroit was stung by the honor of "fattest city" in 2004, *Men's Fitness* depicted the typical Motown resident as, according to *Boston Globe* columnist Ellen Goodman, "a beer-bellied blue-shirted slob eating a bucket of donuts and against a backdrop of—ta da—hub caps."[81] Detroit's mayor—himself a stout fellow—admitted that in his community "We love our cars," attributing communal weight gains to suburbanization and car culture's impact on foodways and exercise patterns. In 2005 a defensive Dallas/Forth Worth television station railed on the magazine's methodology (based in large part on an inventory of doughnut shops, gyms, and health food stores in the yellow pages) and implied an anti-Texas bias. Governing the community dubbed America's "fattest city" in 2005, Houston's own mayor dismissed the *Men's Fitness* rankings as "voodoo and fraud."[82] Even *The Simpsons* ridiculed the body discipline and community embarrassment such rankings inspire. When the Simpsons' hometown of Springfield is named the "World's Fattest Town," it does not share Detroit's or Houston's embarrassment at such a title. Instead, Springfield actually relishes its new status as fattest city, and Homer is relieved that "Now that everyone's so open about being fat, I can finally stop sucking in my gut."[83]

The *Men's Fitness* health measures seem relatively reasonable albeit suggestive ways to assess how communities encourage or dampen healthy lifestyles. However, the doughnut looms transparently in these rankings as a stereotyped symbol of unhealthiness, and the link between doughnut shops and various measures of unhealthiness remains complicated. In 2003 Fort Worth ranked third in the country in *Men's Fitness'* doughnut-shop rankings, trailing Long Beach and Sacramento. While Fort Worth did not fare all that well in the overall ratings, the California doughnut centers did quite well. Sacramento ranked tenth on the fittest list in 2003 and 2004, even though it had the country's second-highest per capita doughnut-shop ranking in 2004. Long Beach still nosed itself into twentieth in 2003 and twenty-third in 2004, despite having a doughnut shop for every nine thousand residents.

The Legislated Doughnut

By the late 1990s a host of public health advocates and politicians began to champion legislation to encourage the consumption of healthy foods, or to at least discourage the consumption of "bad" foods—a list of which often included doughnuts. In 2005, for example, the Texas legislature considered legislation that would add an additional tax on "food not normally considered a major component of a well-balanced meal. If the tax wins approval, buyers of doughnuts, soda, candy, potato chips and such would be paying 10 percent of the price to the government, including the existing 7 percent state sales tax."[84] Presidential candidate Joe Lieberman judiciously avoided championing food taxes, but he did want to include health labels analogous to cigarette health warnings on junk-food advertisements and place nutritional information on menus. These food labels and "Twinkie taxes" borrow from a legislative tradition that has historically produced alcohol codes, smoking laws, and other consumer tariffs to regulate everyday sins. Few of these earlier efforts to discipline commonplace vices have been especially successful, though, unless they made a strong claim to improve public health, which is how smoking legislation succeeded.

The effort to limit smoking and alcohol consumption clearly has had positive effects on public health, and a few less doughnuts would benefit some consumers. Nevertheless, the debate over such taxes is characterized by hyperbole and complicated self-interests. These proposed codes—most have not yet been successfully implemented—are driven by a vast range of material and moral interests that commonly underestimate consumers' commitment to goods like cigarettes and beer or foods like candy, soda, and Ho-Ho's. Drinking, smoking, and even doughnut eating are in some ways transgressive practices that take part of their symbolism from their open defiance of dominant disciplinary codes. These rituals break from a variety of social, moral, and bodily disciplines that various reformers have attempted to police at particular moments. By the late 1950s, for example, there was a swelling tide of evidence that smoking had a significant negative impact on public health, and this awareness drove federal legislation that was hatched in the 1960s. Anti-smoking codes that level stiff tariffs on smokers inspired public health advocates who hoped to fashion similar legislation for high-fat foods. Potato chips, candy, and doughnuts also have a clearly documented negative impact on health, but a distinctive coalition of confection fans, laissez-faire consumer advocates, industrial front groups, and government officials has been wary of such legislation or fought it openly.

Many of the battles to shape the nation's taste buds have been fought in public schools, because schools socialize students to particular foodways and the state can legitimately claim control over school spaces. A stream of worldwide legislation aims to place health warnings or tariffs on certain foods and eliminate others from the hands of students (at least while they are at school). In 2003 and again in 2005, for example, Illinois governor Rod Blagojevich proposed that "junk food" and soda be eliminated from public high school vending machines.[85] A year earlier the New York City School District removed "soda, hard candy, doughnuts, and other junk food from vending machines."[86] For cash-strapped public schools, though, removing soda machines causes a significant loss of revenue. When Governor Arnold Schwarzenegger signed a 2005 bill into California law banning soda sales in high schools, one estimate placed the loss to school revenues at "hundreds of thousands of dollars."[87] Connecticut governor M. Jodi Rell vetoed a similar ban that would have allowed only water, juice, and milk in schools, and similar legislation was rejected or watered down in Kentucky, Arizona, and Oregon.[88]

Despite their success, the soda industry's lobbyists recognized the threat posed by voices such as *Seattle Times* columnist Neal Peirce, who argued that through soda sales "School districts become junk-food pushers." Peirce concluded that a "generation of more obese kids coming out of the schools will spell big trouble later. Smart state governments will give the schools the extra money they need for phys ed and extracurricular activities now. Then they'll ban all soda pop in the schools—saving themselves (and their taxpayers) a real bundle in Medicaid and other health outlays later."[89] In an effort to defuse such rhetoric and turn the tide against anti-soda policies throughout the country, in August 2005 the American Beverage Association announced a new voluntary policy restricting soda sales in schools. The suggested guidelines banned soda sales in elementary schools, allowed soda to be sold only after school in middle schools, and decreed that soda can only be provided in half of all machines in high schools. But *Boston Globe* columnist Derrick Jackson called this a smoke screen, arguing that "Despite its pretense of caring about the nation's youth, the American Beverage Association knows it has hard-wired America to drown the salt and grease with sugar. Some of these burgers, with fries and a large soda, approach or crack the 2,000-calorie barrier."[90]

Efforts to pass such legislation on a federal level have been overwhelmingly unsuccessful. Iowa senator Tom Harkin drafted a federal bill that proposed to develop nationwide nutritional guidelines for foods sold in school vending machines, but it was unable to escape with committee approval.[91] Because schools use à la carte cafeteria sales to cover the losses inflicted by federally subsidized lunch programs, some school boards resist such laws.[92] Nevertheless, in 2002 middle schools in Montgomery County, Maryland, banned all "junk food," which they defined as food with 50 percent or more of its calories coming from fat.[93] At that point the schools' à la carte offerings included doughnuts, Little Debbie cakes, Cheetos, and ice cream bars. The cafeteria manager at one Montgomery County school indicated that she ordered eight dozen doughnuts each day, and they were always popular: "The kids will miss them. I do a lot of doughnuts." Maine passed an especially ambitious anti–junk food law in 2005 that eliminated all soda and candy at school. However, this has been met with criticism by some parents whose candy sales supported organizations including cheerleaders and bands.[94]

The proposed school food changes and junk-food taxes are driven by a complicated combination of sound public health advocacy and desperately underfunded state governments. For many state legislatures, food taxes have become an essential funding source, and more than a dozen states hoped to boost their revenues in 2004 through various food tariffs that might improve public health while they refilled the local coffers.[95] For instance, Detroit mayor Kwame Kilpatrick was saddled with a massive budget as he presided over a community *Men's Fitness* called America's "fattest city" in 2004. He included a 2 percent fast-food tax in his city budget, taking aim at two dilemmas at one time.[96] The New York State legislature considered a proposal to add a .25 percent tax on candy and snacks and eliminate junk food from school vending machines; Washington State hoped to lift a sales tax exemption on candy; and Vermont lawmakers aspired to raise $5 million for education with a 6 percent sales tax on snack foods.[97]

This is not a movement restricted to the United States. In 2003 a Scottish reporter advocated that "foods which are potentially hazardous to health when eaten in excess, because of their high fat, sugar and salt contents should be taxed, applying the same principle as is applied to alcohol."[98] Two years later a clever English entrepreneur began selling the "donut peach," a Spanish fruit that has the shape of an "American doughnut."[99] A supermarket testing sales of the spherical peach packaged them in long boxes that resemble doughnut boxes, and the manager optimistically forecast that "We think kids will love them as they get the fun of a doughnut in a healthy snack."

Doughnut Rights

One observer critical of retailers' power to track the smallest details of consumption through credit and store shopper cards wondered what would happen if "the data eventually gets into the hands of HMOs who might decide to raise premiums on heavy doughnut consumers."[100] For some doughnut consumers and marketers, the threat of surveillance and concrete intervention is often invoked to underscore that consumption is an individual "right" under attack from a variety of hostile forces. American consumer culture has long celebrated individual consumer choice, and as a nation we have been reluctant to impose state restrictions on consumption outside wartime and unusual conditions like oil crises. The state has championed a vast range of voluntary exercise and wellness programs, but many of those are themselves channels for consumption in the form of gym memberships, exercise clothing, plastic surgery, and specialized equipment. Food pyramids and the like have provided federally supervised directions for food consumption for decades, but the state has been less willing to actually tax specific foods as a mechanism to shape food consumption and encroach on our individual consumer choices.

The gulf between an individual's "right" to eat doughnuts and the state's power to impose restrictions is a complicated landscape not easily reduced to right and wrong. In 2003, for instance, the World Health Organization declared obesity a worldwide health epidemic and began drafting a thorough plan for nations confronting obesity. Some observers singled out the report's suggestion that levies could be imposed on producers or consumers of unhealthy foods. The Bush administration declared that such taxes ignored "the notion of personal responsibility," siding with doughnut consumers who consider a trip to the local Dunkin' their "right."[101] A Department of Health and Human Services official wrote to the World Health Organization on behalf of the administration complaining that in many instances its health decrees "are not supported with sufficient scientific evidence."[102]

Not surprisingly, the Center for Consumer Freedom—backed by the restaurant, tobacco, and food industries—champions the ambiguous notion of responsibility and raises suspicions of scientifically backed social engineering. In lockstep with the Bush administration, it defines "consumer freedom" as "the right of adults and parents to choose what they eat, drink, and how they enjoy themselves."[103] This common rhetorical maneuver appeals to many consumers with warm feelings for minor vices like ice cream, steak, or crullers. Rather than advocate a somewhat problematic pro-smoking or "pro-fat" position, the discourse is recast as being about individual freedom to smoke or to eat fattening foods. That "freedom" can be separated from the public health in the mind of many conservatives who argue that individual consumption should not be linked to state-monitored public health at all. The Center for Consumer Freedom is simply among the most vocal groups to attack virtually any state regulation that influences how consumers view products sold by their funders, which in this case includes firms such as Coca-Cola, Wendy's, White Castle, and Tyson Foods. In addition to Wendy's (which owns Tim Hortons), Krispy Kreme has been among the clients of the organization's director, industrial lobbyist Richard Berman.[104]

Alarmed by food regulations and the threat of lawsuits from now-obese customers, the food industry backed the Personal Responsibility in Food Consumption Act, which had the strong support of the Bush administration. The so-called Cheeseburger Bill protected fast-food giants like McDonald's from class-action lawsuits modeled after claims made by smokers. The bill passed in the House in 2004, but the Senate did not vote on the legislation. However, the battleground over such laws simply moved to the states. By 2005 twenty-one state governments had enacted similar laws restricting "obesity lawsuits," and another ten had similar legislation pending. Fast-food chains are not significantly threatened financially by obesity lawsuits, since they are almost non-existent, rarely successful, and unlikely to inflict significant costs on multinationals. However, these corporations are apprehensive of the discovery process in which litigants receive access to company files that might reveal any number of unflattering chain secrets. It seems unlikely that Krispy Kreme will be found to have deliberately targeted consumers with a doughnut "addiction," but there are certainly many secrets that chains would prefer remain private.

There is genuine evidence that "comfort" foods like doughnuts release dopamine, a brain chemical that in one analyst's words makes a consumer "giddy with enjoyment—whether it's brought on by romance or a chocolate doughnut."[105] One study suggested that some consumers have a genetic predisposition to eat foods like doughnuts that are high in fat and sugar.[106] However, linking food choices to biology is often shaky science, and it invariably unsettles the critics of food taxes. A *National Review* columnist, for instance, warned that if genetically based food predispositions are successfully linked to food consumption, it will pave the way for a universe of food taxes: "The only thing we haven't heard yet is about how Big Macs, Mars bars, and Coca-Cola are addictive. I assume studies are underway to prove it, leading inevitably to charges that McDonald's, Hershey, and other purveyors of this poison knew all along and covered it up."[107]

Science likely will demonstrate what many consumers already feel, namely, that for many of us, eating doughnuts or having a cup of coffee is an especially powerful physical experience that is profoundly shaped—but not determined—by biology. Nevertheless, posing this as a threat to free commerce is a transparent rhetorical maneuver. It is clear that many doughnut producers have followed the lead of fast-food chains and the American food industry by pushing large servings and masking some of the more unsavory aspects of their products, regardless of whether such consumption is driven by biological impera-

account of these immigrants' lives somewhat romantically indicated that in "Puerto Rico they snacked on papayas, acerola berries and guava. Now, more often than not, it's Twinkies and doughnuts."[110] The blame for food-related unhealthiness is routinely laid at the feet of a variety of external influences, and doughnuts are often singled out. After a physical revealed that George W. Bush had gained weight during his 2004 presidential campaign, the commander in chief suggested that "I have gone through a campaign where I probably ate too many doughnuts."[111] A 2005 New Zealand study concluded that nearly one in three Kiwi youth was obese, a girth they attributed to advertisements for unhealthy foods. The study argued that 70 percent of outdoor advertising was officially classed by the New Zealand Health Ministry as "unhealthy," identifying the primary offenders as "potato chips, French fries, doughnuts, pies, sweets, sodas, fast food, and iced sweets."[112]

American fast foods certainly contributed to Puerto Rican immigrants' health problems and George Bush's expanding waistline, but the bigger question is why Puerto Rican newcomers and presidential hopefuls embrace mass-produced foods. For many observers the core reason is that consumers become socialized to fast foodways and reflect little on those habits. In 2005, for instance, a Buffalo-area dietician lamented the arrival of several chains to an already-robust local doughnut market, complaining, "I don't know when it became acceptable for us to eat worse than everybody in the rest of the country. We've just developed very bad habits."[113] Krispy Kreme's arrival in London raises the surprisingly maddening question of why people consume doughnuts, and the answer is certainly complex. In October 2003, *Edinburgh Evening News* columnist Margo MacDonald decried the arrival of Krispy Kreme in Harrods. Giddy with their apparent conquest of Harrods, Krispy Kreme had quickly announced plans to soon move into Edinburgh itself. MacDonald, however, was dismayed by the arrival of American food in Scotland, fearing it signaled the British Isles' inevitable descent into obesity. She lamented that by her count 63 percent of Americans are overweight, and "if we learn to love this type of food as much as our transatlantic cousins, we'll soon be as fat as them, too."[114] MacDonald was reduced to puzzlement over why her fellow citizens were migrating toward unhealthy foods. Her concern with public health was not misplaced, but she demonstrated little understanding of what

Many consumers find doughnut display spaces powerful lures to consumption. At Long's Bakery's in south Indianapolis, doughnuts beckon from behind the glass. (Photograph courtesy of Wade Terrell Tharp.)

actually attracted Scottish consumers to Krispy Kreme in particular and doughnuts in general.

In an even more damning critique of doughnuts, *Scotland on Sunday* columnist Alex Massie looked beyond the likelihood that doughnuts would add to the national paunch and instead probed the impact of doughnut marketing and consumption on health, nationalism, and state economy.[115] Massie argued that Krispy Kreme heralds an especially insidious conquest of the healthy world by American food producers. Assessing Krispy Kreme and Dunkin Donuts' competition in Edinburgh, he decried "'calorie colonialism' planned by corporate America." Questioning the impact of American corporate chains on Scotland's economy, Massie quoted a London professor's lament that "At a time when Britain is slowly waking up to the enormous problem of obesity, and the immense social and financial cost of diet-related disease, it's ironic for the heartlands of the fat culture [i.e., the United States] to continue to send over unwelcome additions to an obesogenic food environment." Pushing beyond the specter of a Scottish citizenry gorging on doughnuts, Massie suggested that the doughnut chains were symptomatic of American food-manufacturing patterns that produced too much food for domestic consumption. Foreign markets were economically necessary to doughnut manufacturers' profits, and the reach of global capitalism would inevitably have a profound social and material effect on Scotland.

"Highly Educated People Dunking Doughnuts": Doughnuts at Work and School

Some workplaces have long encouraged sedentism and provided fattening food—stereotypically doughnuts—to munch on during the day. The caricature of a doughnut consumer is of a working-class stiff, but a *Nightly Business Report* columnist suggested that swelling obesity rates were actually the fault of an office laboring class "led by highly educated people dunking doughnuts and stuffing their faces while hunched over computer screens."[116] There is no clear evidence that office culture in itself has led to a spiraling obesity rate, but a number of observers have offered their advice for how to change office life, which typically includes eliminating doughnuts. For instance, the *Sacramento Bee*'s formula for a healthy workplace involved replacing "doughnuts, coffee and sodas with 100 percent fruit or vegetable juice, fruits, vegetables and whole grain bagels." One California legislator even suggested that doughnuts were partly to blame for bad legislation. When he first arrived at the Senate, "junk food such as doughnuts and 'mega-muffins' were the only things available in the snack room. 'No wonder we were going on energy highs and crashing and getting irritable and turning out terrible legislation . . . that was skewed by our roller coaster of insulin and sugar highs and sugar lows.'"[117]

Many workplaces have launched wellness programs that have had profoundly positive effects on their workforce, but some employers have found that doughnut consumers provide formidable resistance. In 2005, for instance, Boston city councilor Michael Ross championed a city hall exercise program aspiring to make city employees eat healthier. A Boston journalist wondered if it was actually possible to create a "doughnut-free zone in Boston's City Hall," because there "were some doughnuts still lying around the office." A city employee sniffed that the Ross would be compelled to "give me a good reason, otherwise I'll eat more [doughnuts]." Another employee complained, "I listen to my stomach, and it says 'I want a blueberry doughnut.' That's what it's telling me and I have to have it. He [Councilor Ross] doesn't have to have them, but I want one."[118]

Despite the persistent criticism of doughnuts, they are especially powerful socializing mechanisms. For instance, public schools have long mulled over ways they can involve fathers in their children's schooling, and some have discovered that doughnuts might have a positive effect. Mothers are stereotypically considered the primary parent administering their children's education, so mothers long ago assumed the most prominent roles in parent-teacher organizations and among school volunteers. Yet throughout the country clever school administrators apparently determined at more or less the same moment that doughnuts could provide a powerful magnet to lure absentee fathers to school. These "Doughnuts with Dad" breakfasts have been conducted by schools throughout the nation, and they normally involve some moment in the morning that a father and his student child sit together in the cafeteria munching a doughnut. A Winchester, Virginia, school's doughnut breakfast drew more than eighty fathers, many of whom admitted that the prospect of doughnuts added to the event's attraction. One father indicated that he was happy "as long as they keep the doughnuts coming."[119] In Columbia, Missouri, when Paxton Keeley Elementary School hoped to lure fathers to help with school volunteering it had a "Donuts for Dads" breakfast. One Keeley father acknowledged that "The free doughnut got me here."[120]

The ultimate mission is of course to bring dads into the fold. A Detroit "Donuts and Dads" breakfast drew more than 230 people, and the principal admitted that "There was an underlying agenda to exposing more men to the types of programs that they can get involved with to help support" the school. He conceded that "one of the things we need to do is find nontraditional ways to get parents involved."[121] When Florida mandated a "Dad's Week" in the public schools, several schools included a doughnut breakfast as a central event.[122] An East St. Louis, Illinois, "Donuts and Dads" program cast its doughnut breakfasts as "male bonding sessions," a common sentiment in such programs elsewhere that aspire to connect fathers with male students and advocate for the influence of men in children's lives.[123]

While the "Doughnuts with Dad" programs have received little or no critique, the doughnut's position in other school programs has been more problematic. Some school systems and doughnut producers have offered doughnut incentive awards to students who receive good grades or reach particular standards. In Palm Beach, for instance, Krispy Kreme offered up free doughnuts to any students receiving A's on their report cards.[124] Krispy Kreme hatched the promotion itself and sent letters to district principals that provided details on the promotion. The "doughnuts-for-A's" program offered class field trips to local doughnut shops, and Krispy Kreme provided classroom posters of doughnuts that students could decorate with "success sprinkles." Krispy Kreme's Florida promotion linking scholastic success with doughnuts instantly drew a torrent of national attacks. "I certainly would not want to see posters in classrooms with doughnuts on them as a reminder every day, day in and day out," complained one observer. "When you do well and reward yourself with food, there is something that will continue to promote obesity." A national columnist concluded: "I hope that principals in Palm Beach . . . will decline the doughnut maker's transparent attempt to sugarcoat its image." When a local Krispy Kreme spokesperson was asked if the company had considered the potential health impacts of doughnut consumption, she somewhat clumsily admitted, "As far as I know there's been no concern on my end."[125]

The concern for students' health is perhaps well intentioned, but doughnuts seem singled out among many problematic school foods. Restaurant chains offering up pizza, ice cream, and other equally fattening foods quietly provide similar promotions to students all over the country with relatively little protest, and a legion of bands and baseball teams have hawked Krispy Kremes at school for decades without reservation. One Krispy Kreme defender pointed out that even the highest-achieving student would not be eating all that many doughnuts: "If children today got as much excercise [sic] as they SHOULD be (put DOWN the gameboy and go OUTSIDE!) then getting rewarded with

Krispy Kreme donuts for good grades would not be a big health concern. . . . But it's SIX donuts (at the most) every NINE WEEKS. . . . This reward program is NOT going to cause a healthy kid to have weight problems."[126]

Teachers who capitalize on the doughnut's popularity are subjected to similar critique. In Bowling Green, Kentucky, for example, a high school principal picked classrooms at random and informed them that if the teacher could successfully answer three questions the class would receive doughnuts. The local paper diplomatically applauded the principal's effort to provide educational incentives but concluded that "at a time when we are trying to cut back on junk food in our schools and combat obesity among our youths, we don't think that doughnuts are the best reward to give to our students."[127] Doughnuts can also be used to penalize bad behavior outside classrooms. After cell phones continually disturbed sessions of the South Dakota legislature, it was decreed that anybody whose phone rang during a committee session would be required to bring in doughnuts for the committee. One lobbyist recovering from a heart attack conceded that "deep-fried doughnuts may not be the best reward for legislators. 'Doughnuts are terrible for them.'"[128]

Doughnuts at Church

Church gatherings have long featured doughnuts at their after-service buffets and Bible-study groups. "Christ said we are to love one another," according to the Reverend Gene Beezer, of Faith Bible Fellowship in Santee, California. "If you never eat together, can it be said that you love one another?" As Reverend Beezer recognized, sharing food is at the heart of many churches' socialization, where food bonding canvasses everything from vast Sunday-dinner spreads to morning-meeting doughnuts. Gluttony is the target of disdain if not outright sinfulness in many faiths, but it has rarely secured the same surveillance as sins like sexual promiscuousness or alcohol consumption. The noted theologian and doughnut aficionado Homer Simpson even argues that "If God didn't want us to eat in church, he'd have made gluttony a sin."[129]

There is some evidence that evangelicals—especially Baptists—have led the march from pew to dining room, but doughnuts appear in a wide range of faith-based socializing.[130] Food has been a staple of church socializing for many of the same reasons that it binds people at fraternal lodges, PTO meetings, and a legion of other social gatherings. Sharing food is an especially intimate, nurturing experience shared between people, so food rituals can establish powerful relationships. Religious communities magnify this effect, because sharing faith is typically a more intimate bond than the relationship between two PTO committees or neighbors at a block picnic. The Vineyard Church of Ithaca, New York, for instance, serves coffee and doughnuts during the service because they "believe that fellowship is an important aspect of being in church. So we give time during the service for people to get a cup of coffee and meet someone they don't know."[131]

Discussions of doughnuts in church typically refer to the ambiguous relaxation doughnuts engender. For instance, the "Cowboy Church" in Lafayette, Georgia, attempts to create a distinctive, tranquil atmosphere by meeting in a barn, dressing casually, and providing comfort food to the congregants. One young visitor admitted, "I like the doughnuts."[132] A *Focus on the Family* writer eager to school his son's peers on faith noted that he "had the privilege of meeting with my two sons' eight best friends for doughnuts and Bible study almost every week during middle and high school. We would discuss their most pressing issues and apply Scripture and prayer to their challenges."[133] One woman even argues that her break from a congregation "happened over doughnuts. I had made a 'commitment' to bring doughnuts to a Sunday morning fellowship. On Saturday night my husband became ill. I called Susie and asked if someone else could get the doughnuts. . . . Well, you would have thought I'd broken a salt covenant with God himself. I was so thoroughly reamed. . . . I just never went back."[134] Doughnuts may have won this reputation because they are seen as special foods, even at richly stocked church buffet tables. However, they also may relax consumers because the doughnut is a rather prosaic comfort food being eaten while contemplating the most profound questions of faith.

Doughnuts occasionally make appearances in churches' community evangelism. On Christmas Eve each year the Vineyard Community Church near Cincinnati gives away thousands of Krispy Kreme doughnuts. "I think if Jesus was here, he'd be out doing this kind of thing," the pastor suggested, indicating that he had "seen people cry when they receive the doughnuts."[135] Like their Vineyard colleagues in the Midwest, the Vineyard Church of Richmond, Virginia, developed a community-service ministry in which members perform everyday tasks for their neighbors. The congregants told a local paper that they do mostly commonplace jobs as part of their service, such as washing the windows at a local drugstore, providing fresh fruit to homeless people, or cleaning the bathrooms at a gay bar (although the bar's staff did not remember the ministry ever cleaning their toilets). Among these somewhat mundane favors for neighbors, the ministry has given doughnuts to local college students. When students question the congregants' motivation, one church member says, "I'll just tell them God loves you. He wants you to have a doughnut."[136] When an Ohio missionary set up shop across the street from an area where prostitutes marketed their product, he was not "sure how he was going to minister to the people in the neighborhood, but God began to open the doors of ministry. 'A local doughnut shop gave us their leftover pastries. . . . We started handing them out to the prostitutes and people on the streets.'"[137]

Despite God's call to the doughnut counter, some churches have concluded that socializing over food has produced expanding congregational waistbands and significant health dilemmas. This seems to be especially problematic among southern working-class churches, which wrestle with a deep-seated regional favor for fried and sweet foods as well as historically modest education on public health issues like obesity. A 1997 Southern Baptist Convention survey found that 60 percent of its ministers and their spouses were overweight, another 47 percent were obese, and 61 percent acknowledged that they ate doughnuts and pastries.[138] A 2006 study found that there was a significantly elevated rate of obesity among women in Baptist congregations, and among Baptists, African Americans and congregants with limited education tended to have particularly high rates of obesity.[139]

One typical Texas pastor plied his flock with doughnuts for years, but he came to believe that the church should encourage food discipline like that extended to alcohol, adultery, or drugs: "People loved the Krispy Kremes, but the more we started thinking about this, we were saying, 'We can't talk about this on the one hand and on the other hand have all these doughnuts.'" A significant wave of diet tomes in this vein have appeared that model diets on the Bible, such as *The Maker's*

Diet and *What Would Jesus Eat?* Jordan Rubin's *Maker's Diet* singles out pre-sermon coffee and doughnuts as a church-based consumption pattern that diverges from the image of healthiness painted in the Bible. Some churches have defined this as a moral issue broader than individual body discipline. The newsletter for the Lutheran Network for Inclusive Vision wondered, "What if all of our members were to make the coffee and doughnuts sacrifice once a week?"[140] Multiplying the 1,297 members at the moment by two dollars a week over a full year, they envisioned "a magnificent Network fund of $134,888!" This moral choice between individual consumption desire and collective needs is routinely directed at a variety of commodities that appear to be interfering with some measure of good work. The network column concluded that forsaking doughnuts and coffee for service would reinforce the Corinthians passage "For why should my liberty be determined by another person's scruples?"

The Doughnut-Addicted Bear

Perhaps the most curious moral discourse involving doughnuts revolves around a practice known as bearbaiting. The term *bearbaiting* refers to a host of strategies used to attract bears to a hunter's location. Baiting is done with foods bears find especially attractive, and bears return to a baited location where a hunter eventually lies in wait. In a typical bearbaiting, a hole is cut into a large drum so that the bear will be able to reach in and eat the food, and if it enjoys the fare it will return on subsequent days to an awaiting hunter. The materials used to bait bears vary, but bears apparently delight in doughnuts, in addition to grease, rotting fruit, and meat. When Washington State Department of Fish and Wildlife wardens trapped a bear (that was subsequently released elsewhere), the marauder was lured into a trap baited with Krispy Kremes because, according to one warden, "It works well."[141]

For some observers, bearbaiting violates ethical hunting, or what hunters call "fair chase." In 2004 the electorates of Maine and Alaska considered legislation that proposed to outlaw the practice. In the debate leading up to the ballot initiatives, doughnuts' role in baiting was routinely invoked. When former Minnesota governor Jesse Ventura was asked for his position on bearbaiting, he indicated that "Going out there and putting jelly doughnuts down and Yogi comes up and sits there and thinks he's found the mother lode for five days in a row—and then you back-shoot him from a tree? . . . That ain't sport, that's assassination."[142] Another suggested that "taking out a bear on its doughnut run sounds like waiting at the 7-Eleven to shoot your neighbor."[143] One bearbaiting opponent argued that "there is something especially wicked in a policy that turns them [bears] into donut addicts, only to be shot at point-blank range."[144]

Much of the bearbaiting debate revolved around how hunters' use of doughnuts revealed their character shortcomings. Baiting opponents painted themselves as defenders of pristine wilderness who were advocating fair play, and they recurrently brought up doughnuts as a rhetorical mechanism to demean bearbaiting hunters. One Maine baiting critic, for instance, wondered, "How fulfilling is it to shoot a bear with its head in a barrel of jelly donuts?"[145] In Alaska an observer attacked bait food as debasing to nature itself when he wondered, "Stale doughnuts, lard, honey-drenched dog food—is this any kind of meal for a wild Alaska bear?" Another characterized bearbaiting fare as "a typical mall rat diet. . . . So when supporters of Question 2 [the proposal to ban baiting] say 'bears shouldn't be shot over a pile of jelly donuts,' they are certainly right about the doughnuts part."[146] It is unclear if baiting would be more acceptable if traps were baited with granola and brie, but the implication seems to be that hunters defending this practice were slothful, overweight, and undereducated, which is a lot like the caricature of doughnut consumers.

The reality in Maine was that bearbaiting hunters were not unrefined backwoodsmen who used their stale doughnuts to bag bears. Much of the bearbaiting in Maine was done by local guides who use doughnuts and other foods to attract future trophies for wealthy hunters. One Maine observer characterized these bear hunters as part of a vacationing stream of "affluent Bostonians and tourists from points south and west" who "come to Maine to climb the mountains, see the coast, eat the lobster, buy antiques, and, yes, kill things."[147] A *Portland Phoenix* columnist conceded this, but he still got in a dig on doughnuts when he noted that "hunters pay hefty fees to wait for the animals, usually in tree stands set above barrels of Dunkin' Donuts and other fatty foods."[148] The business of guiding bear hunts is worth roughly $7 million a year by one measure, though pro-hunting groups estimate that its value is exponentially higher when hunters' economic impact in hotels, restaurants, and local businesses is added to paying a guide.[149] Consequently, the guides and Maine's Department of Inland Fisheries and Wildlife both mounted stiff resistance to the effort to outlaw bearbaiting, and the measure was defeated. It also was defeated in Alaska, so many bears continue to feast on doughnuts as an ill-fated final meal.

Marrying Krispy Kreme

Many newlyweds now cement their nuptials by serving doughnuts to their guests or constructing doughnut wedding cakes. While the phenomenon has won considerable media attention since the late 1990s, doughnuts have been making appearances at weddings since the nineteenth century. In 1869, for instance, the *Brooklyn Eagle* reported that after a "dazzling" wedding a "feast of reason and a flow of whisky followed. The table was loaded with luxuries. Piles of ham-sandwiches, and plates of doughnuts, pig's feet and pickled muscles, with clam chowder hot."[150] This would make for a rather distinctive reception buffet today, but doughnut fans have recently elevated doughnuts from the reception buffet and begun to make their wedding cakes from artfully arranged doughnuts. The vast majority of these wedding cakes are fashioned from Krispy Kremes. It is not especially surprising that former CEO Scott Livengood had a Krispy Kreme cake at his 2003 wedding, much like the one his mother had made for his birthday thirty-four years before.[151] Four years earlier a Krispy Kreme accountant also was married over a doughnut cake, one of the earliest references to the doughnut cakes.[152] However, many people with no comparable material commitment to the chain arrange mountains of doughnuts—almost always Krispy Kremes—to reign over their symbolically important first matrimonial meal. One self-described "Krispy Kreme freak" made her own wedding cake out of Krispy Kremes, and even she was surprised at the volume of interest in her blog's directions helping others reproduce the creation.[153] At least one baker in Tampa offered to prepare Krispy Kreme doughnut cakes for those who wanted a professional's guidance.

For some of the dearly beloveds contemplating the Krispy Kreme cakes, the doughnut cake is a tactic that evades overpriced cakes and increasingly expensive ceremonies without sacrificing the essential decadence of a wedding cake. Viewed this way, the doughnut wedding cake critiques the overblown and overpriced ceremonies that are championed by a huge industry producing wedding commodities including clothing, pictures, and cakes. In the labyrinthine world of wedding planning, cakes are a significant expense that cost an average of six dollars a slice, but "Krispy Kreme freak's" cake cost only about one hundred dollars. In a move to join a phalanx of wedding advisers, the Krispy Kreme corporate offices immediately began to advertise an adviser who was available to consult couples preparing a Krispy Kreme cake.[154] However, their advice appears to have revolved around construction techniques, since the shops simply sell the doughnuts and the actual cake assembly is done by the bride and groom or some especially devoted family members. Many couples' doughnut cakes attempt to reproduce conventional wedding-cake style. For instance, "Krispy Kreme freak" dusted her doughnut cake with powdered sugar, preserving the Victorian tradition of a white wedding cake to symbolize purity. Yet others recognize the doughnut cake as a clear statement defying the commonplace expectation that a wedding is so special that it requires outrageous expense to create a unique experience. One couple embraced the anti-bourgeois class dimensions of a doughnut wedding cake by constructing a Krispy Kreme cake with a Jack Daniels fountain. In 2002 an issue of *In Style* included pictures of a doughnut wedding cake, *Time* reported on the phenomenon, and cable channels followed. The doughnuts also began to appear in mitzvahs, since Krispy Kremes are kosher. In January 2005 a Jewish trade association built a colossal doughnut wedding cake made from 1,818 doughnuts arranged in a five-foot, three-inch pyramid, which a reporter pointed out accounted for 363,600 calories.[155] (However, this fell well short of the record cake assembled by Krispy Kreme in July 2002, a colossal mountain of fried dough containing 14,832 doughnuts and weighing 2,413 pounds).[156]

Couples who are reluctant to forsake a traditional wedding cake altogether can still make Krispy Kreme part of their ceremony. A St. Petersburg couple had a conventional wedding cake, but as guests left the reception a Krispy Kreme salesman and his basset hound handed out little boxes containing two doughnuts. "I can't tell you how many times I've left a wedding reception and gone to a drive-through," the bride explained. "People are hungry after all that dancing."[157] Although Krispy Kreme has dominated the media coverage of doughnut weddings, certainly many more newly married couples celebrate at their own favorite doughnut haunts. One blogger celebrated a friend's Indianapolis wedding with "Long's donuts, Clementine oranges, and champagne."[158] A Texas couple tied the knot with a conventional cake, but the following morning "everyone enjoyed a decadent doughnut breakfast followed by a flashback to Dawn and Paul's first date—clay shooting."[159]

Some especially devoted doughnut fans even commit themselves in the doughnut shop itself. Voodoo Doughnuts in Portland, Oregon, began hosting weddings in 2003; $175 gets doughnuts and coffee for ten. Since the shop's proprietors are ordained by the Universal Life Church, the wedding is truly legally binding (the shop even offers Swahili lessons as part of its range of services not likely offered by a marketer in any business).[160] In New York and Philadelphia, Dunkin' Donuts offered two wedding packages in its "Hole-y Matrimony Contest."[161] Dunkin' set up a web page at which couples could recount stories about how they proposed, and six stories were selected for a popular vote to determine the two winners in each market. The two couples were married in February 2005 in tents outside Dunkin' shops in the two cities.

The Popular Doughnut

Tim Horton is perhaps the most famous person to add his name to doughnuts, but a number of celebrities have hawked doughnuts. Mickey Lolich, for instance, pitched the Detroit Tigers to a World Series win in 1968. In Detroit, Lolich won a reputation for being a likable "regular guy" and was sometimes chided for being a portly fellow who referred to himself as "the beer drinker's idol."[162] Two years after Lolich had left the Tigers in 1975, a *Detroit News* writer noted that "there was ample midsection that showed through Lolich's uniform and belied his pitching ability," snidely noting that Lolich "didn't change after he retired from baseball and opened a donut shop."[163] Lolich did indeed become a partner in a doughnut shop near the end of his baseball career, and after retiring he became the owner of a suburban Detroit shop in 1979.[164] Like many other athletes who have gone into business after their career, Lolich understood that "everybody wants to meet you because you're a ballplayer," although he did really work in the shop nearly every day.[165]

Most of the famous-name franchisees like Jimmy Buffet (who owns a Palm Beach Krispy Kreme) have very little everyday oversight of their stores and tend to see their businesses as elements in broad investment strategies. Dick Clark, for example, partnered in the firm that owns Krispy Kreme franchise rights in the United Kingdom, and he also managed an eponymous American Bandstand restaurant chain.[166] Clark, who was diagnosed with diabetes in 1994, would seem an unlikely partner in a doughnut chain, but his powerful connection to 1950s America makes him a very effective symbol for a firm like Krispy Kreme.[167] In Atlanta, Krispy Kreme awarded a franchise to the recently dethroned home run king Hank Aaron, an especially diversified businessman with stakes in a series of fast-food franchises including Church's, Popeye's, and Arby's as well as auto dealerships. Other celebrity doughnut shops aspire to unusually lofty goals. José Iglesias and his wife own Mac's Doughnuts, an independent Lavonia, Georgia, doughnut shop. Iglesias used the shop's profits to contribute to what he imagines will become a multicultural "Bible center."

The doughnut's trail through popular culture has been most eloquently blazed by Homer Simpson, whose overpowering love for the variety doughnut may qualify him as the pastry's patron saint. Homer's attraction to doughnuts exploits working-class stereotypes in much the same way as his overall persona; that is, Homer works slowly, is likable but incompetent, and milks doughnut breaks while he avoids exercise and erudition. Springfield's number one cop, Clancy Wiggum, also caricatures the stereotypical cop. The gargantuan Chief Wiggum is a slow-witted and lazy policeman always in search of comfort foods ranging from chocolate bananas to doughnuts. The *Simpsons* characters are creatures of desire, and Homer's doughnut yearnings illuminate a familiar clash between desire and discipline. For Homer this clash is usually won by desire. For instance, when co-worker Lenny delivers the day's doughnuts to the nuclear plant's break room, Homer determines "I can't spend all my life eating" and resolves to have just one plain cake doughnut. However, when Lenny and Carl try to convince him to join them, Homer quickly relents and declares, "Maybe I'll have three or ten of those jumbo triple-glaze deals there."[168] Even Homer's dreams often involve doughnuts. One episode opens with Homer dreaming about a beauty pageant at which an announcer intones that a contestant shaped like a doughnut with fetching female legs is a "vision in raspberry cream." Conflating carnal and food desires, Homer drools that this is "Pure genius."[169]

The Simpsons sounds a complicated position on real-life body ideologies and legal efforts to influence food consumption. Much of the show displays how the likes of Homer, Chief Wiggum, Barney Gumble, and their neighbors are comforted by beer, candy, doughnuts, and other consumable vices, so The Simpsons champions an everyday politics that respects such desire. Springfield engages in the same introspection that many real communities have facing public health challenges. When Marge realizes the marketplace is overwhelmingly oriented to unhealthy foods, she aspires to introduce legislation that will introduce alternatives. Instead of sugar-free doughnuts, for instance, Quik-E-Mart manager Apu offers "sugar, free donuts," explaining that each box comes with doughnuts *and* free sugar. These products all come from the "Motherloving Sugar Corporation," so Marge launches a class-action suit that uncovers the firm's injection of addictive chemicals into its products, including "Choco-Blasted Baby Aspirin" and "Honey-Glazed Cauliflower." Marge's legislation eliminates all forms of sugar and shutters the local doughnut shop, Lard Lad. Ultimately, though, the law becomes unenforceable and is repealed, leading Marge to conclude, "I guess you just can't use the law to nag. Maybe I should just stop trying to change the world." This position is relatively typical of the cartoon's complicated social critiques. On the one hand, the failure of Marge's law is in keeping with The Simpsons' general wariness of the state. The show has lampooned legislative efforts to regulate various dimensions of everyday life ranging from media to alcohol consumption. On the other hand, Marge voices a commonplace discomfort with multinationals and a feeling of consumer powerlessness in the face of firms like Lard Lad and Krusty Burger.

In The Simpsons' hands, doughnuts are an especially powerful mechanism to examine the limits of desire, since doughnuts seem to have no significant redeeming feature besides the pleasure their ingestion induces. Even the standard variety doughnut with sprinkles is not always enough to satisfy Homer. In one episode, Homer creates his own "variety doughnut" at Apu's by adding M&M's, Jolly Ranchers, a Twizzler, and a Mounds bar.[170] Apu notes that these candies are not sprinkles: "Perhaps in Shangri-La they are, but not in here." Homer's desire for doughnuts is even more powerful than his personal pride. When Homer gets a helper monkey, the chimp escapes to the top of a telephone pole with Homer's doughnuts, leaving Homer to curse him from the ground. When the chimp throws a half-eaten doughnut to the ground, Homer initially refuses it but quickly relents and eats the chimp's discard.[171]

Homer's devotion to doughnuts often is depicted as an unquenchable desire with powerful potential consequences. In a fit of doughnut hunger, for instance, Homer sells his soul to the Devil for a doughnut, but he is warned that finishing the doughnut will seal his fate. Homer sets aside the final bite, but even knowing the consequences of eating it, he is unable to resist the forbidden last bite. The Devil ends up losing his case to claim Homer's soul, but Satan turns Homer's head into a doughnut as a penalty. As Homer eats his own pastry head—perhaps the ultimate show of desire as the consumer eats himself—Marge pleads with him not to pick at his doughnut head, yet Homer complains, "I'm so sweet and tasty."[172]

When Homer is sent to Hell to face an apparently ironic fate of eating doughnuts incessantly, the Devil's assistants are frustrated to find that Simpson's doughnut desire knows no bounds. "I don't understand it," laments the Devil's fiendish assistant. "James Coco went mad in fifteen minutes."[173] When Homer has a nightmare about his ultimate fate, he sees himself in a court populated by giant doughnut people who accuse him of "eating half of the population of the planet of the doughnuts." Standing in chains before a judge, Homer fails to show regret and actually eats a bite of his defense attorney. When Homer awakes he finds that while he slept all but one of the break room's doughnuts were eaten. Homer decides to place that final doughnut in the nuclear reactor, envisioning that it will produce a vastly enlarged super-doughnut, but he simply ends up setting fire to the reactor.[174]

Homer's primary local doughnut shop is Lard Lad, which is topped by a monstrous doughnut-toting man who looks a lot like Big Boy. Homer refers to Lard Lad as "the chain that put the fat in fat Southern sheriffs."[175] In one episode he steals Lard Lad's signature colossal steel doughnut, and when Lard Lad is animated by a freak storm he pursues Homer to retrieve the doughnut. When the First Church of Springfield incorporates advertising in the chapel, a Lard Lad statue is prominently displayed in the church.[176] Even Krusty Burger sells doughnuts, although its offering is a "doughnut burger with cheese."[177]

The line between popular culture and reality is often murky, so it should not be surprising that *The Simpsons* bleeds over into everyday reality in odd ways. For instance, two *Simpsons* fans won a contest to visit Homer and Marge's hometown of Springfield, which does not really exist, so the contest's organizers at Fox-UK flew the two Yorkshire fans to Springfield, Illinois, as a stand-in. From the list of Springfields scattered throughout the country, the Illinois namesake was chosen because "There was more sort of opportunity in Illinois because of the doughnut factory and the high school."[178] The men toured the Mel-O-Cream doughnut plant and agreed afterward that in choosing between British doughnuts and the American version "There's no comparison." For those fans with a powerful attraction to Lard Lad Donuts a play-set was released in 2001 for use with a universe of *Simpsons'* themed figures. Homer's doughnut attraction has even found its way onto the editorial page. In 1999 Homer's attraction to doughnuts and his pet exclamation "D'oh!" were used by a *Pittsburgh Post-Gazette* political cartoonist to ridicule security at Los Alamos National Laboratory. The lab had been the victim of espionage, and the cartoon showed Homer eating a doughnut in the security booth and proclaiming "D'oh!" as an ICBM is hauled away. An "interview" with Homer Simpson in *FHM* (i.e., *For Him Magazine*) asked Homer if he exercised. He indicated that he lifted weights, like furniture, but "it all depends what my doughnut has rolled under."[179] The most stunning intersection of popular culture and reality may have come in 1992, when an eight-year-old San Francisco boy choking on an orange was saved when his sister administered the Heimlich maneuver. She claimed to have learned the technique from a *Simpsons* episode in which, after hurriedly eating doughnuts and gagging, Homer gives himself the Heimlich maneuver.

Doughnuts at the Movies

Doughnuts have recurrently appeared in the movies since the 1914 Charlie Chaplin film *Dough and Dynamite,* also known as *The Doughnut Designer.* In 1936 *Doughnuts and Society* spun the story of two women who run a doughnut shop and find their children in a relationship. Doughnuts and doughnut shops also made prominent supporting appearances in many films and television shows, including the 1966 feature *A Funny Thing Happened on the Way to the Forum* and the 1990–91 television show *Twin Peaks.* The 1998 feature film *Primary Colors,* for instance, tells a story of a southern politician modeled on Bill Clinton who has a powerful fondness for women and doughnuts. Krispy Kreme has found a way to insinuate itself into a vast range of films, making an appearance in *Barbershop, Bruce Almighty, Collateral Damage, Hitch, How to Lose a Guy in 10 Days,* and *Mr. Deeds.* Their appearance in *Blade II*—a vampire movie in which the sidekick loves Krispy Kremes—shows how broadly a brand can be marketed. The link between vampires and doughnuts actually had already been established in the 1995 Canadian feature *Blood & Donuts,* in which a recently awakened vampire stumbles into an all-night doughnut shop and begins a relationship with one of the shop's waitresses.

The most interesting feature film involving doughnuts and their moralized meanings may be the 2004 movie *Harold and Kumar Go to White Castle,* which ultimately does not include doughnuts at all. The film depicts the voyage of two stoners seeking a White Castle. Most chains micromanage brand symbolism, so linking White Castle's trademark "sliders" (i.e., little hamburgers) with marijuana consumption is a somewhat challenging brand relationship. Nevertheless, White Castle's marketing director believed there was "something authentic in the way the script described how people feel about our distinctive taste and the lengths they'll go to."[180] This might well describe how some people feel about Krispy Kreme, under the influence or not. Appropriately, the film originally was to include two friends who were simultaneously searching for a Krispy Kreme to satisfy their own marijuana-induced hunger. Unlike White Castle, though, Krispy Kreme was unwilling to overlook Harold and Kumar's drug consumption and did not allow the firm to appear in the movie. The effort to manage brand symbolism is already difficult, but to then aspire to define the doughnut's very symbolism is nearly hopeless.

The moral quandaries revolving around doughnuts are socially interested efforts to restrict a good's symbolism, which is typical of the debates over any contested good. Such discussions waged in public discourse or forged through legislation have typically had an uneven impact on the consumption of such goods, but they have had a genuine impact on how we socially define such things: we may acknowledge that the doughnut is somehow bad for us, but many of us we find ways to consume them anyway. Doughnuts have found their way into discussion ranging from diets to the movies because they have such broad and contested meaning.

Conclusion

The quintessentially American food, the doughnut can today be consumed almost anywhere in the world. What those fried dough spheres mean in any given place and moment can differ quite a bit, but the deepest social significance of doughnuts typically passes without comment from the many people who make and eat doughnuts. It is not really all that surprising that a rather consequential thing might be greeted by an apparently contradictory silence. Doughnuts are especially prosaic things, and when they occupy our attention they tend to be targets for sarcasm rather than reflections of consequential social sentiments.

Nevertheless, food is a complicated thing that is difficult to understand in isolation from a vast range of cultural, economic, and personal factors that vary from one time and place to another. Doughnuts are selective mirrors of roughly two hundred years of foodways that cannot be understood without assessing the complexities of marketing, mass production, body disciplines, and suburbanization, among other things. And if we dig just a little bit we can see that doughnuts loom in many public discussions that have no clear connection to fried dough.

It is not all that surprising that doughnuts are seen as both sacraments of faith as well as symbols of our utter lack of discipline. It is not essential that we settle this symbolic quandary and resolve precisely what doughnuts "really" mean, because this does not appear to be possible. Instead, the most profitable way to understand doughnuts—if not most material culture—is as distorted mirrors of ourselves, ways in which we obliquely discuss our identities, communities, and culture.

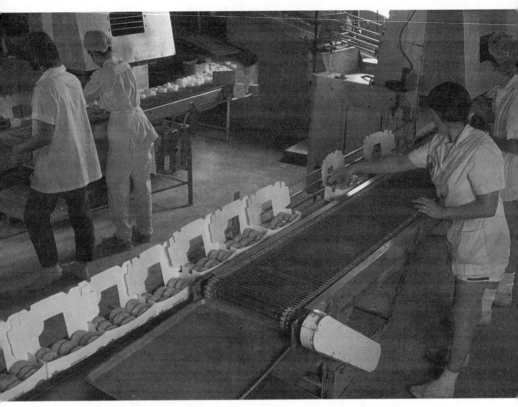

Many doughnut shops aspire to reach beyond the walls of the bakery and have turned to mass production to market their products. (Photograph © Najlah Feanny/CORBIS SABA.)

The doughnut is not a clear historical document of American life so much as it is an insight into who we have imagined ourselves to be and how we have seen ourselves over two centuries. Foods like doughnuts are wrapped in an especially complex symbolism that accommodates the sentiments of many different consumers, so we tend to project our aspirations and ambitions onto those commodities.

Consuming doughnuts provides ways we can imagine community in new forms, rethink ethnic and cultural identity, and perhaps even empower ourselves. It is not completely clear, though, that doughnuts are capable of pulling off such miraculous feats as forging a more meaningful "doughnut-shop culture," elevating regional cultural identity, or resisting dominant bodily disciplines in ways that can be considered completely empowering. Ultimately, doughnut shops are still commodity marketplaces designed to secure our labor power; as a massproduced food, doughnuts do not really make a very strong case for a particularly clear ethnic or regional heritage; and if we choose to defy some bodily disciplines, doughnuts will deliver us a host of significant health problems.

This does not make doughnuts any less consequential. It simply means that they are conflicted in the same way as most of the material things that surround us. It is a quite meaningful conflict, because it negotiates opposing notions of nationalism, body discipline, and class, among many other things. The experience of eating doughnuts, lingering over a cruller, and sharing deep-fried concoctions with family and friends is also powerful, so like our most beloved foods, the doughnut is both a complicated mirror into ourselves and society just as it provides a fine-grained vision of our desires and identities. As Homer Simpson intones, "Doughnuts: Is there anything they can't do?"

Notes

Chapter 1. "The Church of Krispy Kreme"

1. Nora Ephron, "Sugar Babies," *The New Yorker: From the Archives*, August 12, 2002, http://www.newyorker.com/archive/content/?020819fr_archive05.

2. Curtis Sittenfeld, "Minister of Culture," *Fast Company* 17 (1998): 64.

3. Roy Blount Jr., "Southern Comfort," *New York Times*, September 8, 1996, SM67.

4. Candace Comb, "Eight Foods That Really Are Evil," *Shape*, August 2003, http://www.findarticles.com/p/articles/mi_m0846/is_12_22/ai_104943689.

5. Mary MacVean, "Krazy Kravings," *Salon*, March 10, 2000, http://dir.salon.com/travel/food/feature/2000/03/10/kreme/index.html.

6. Derek Robins, "Doughnuts Disturb Wilson," *Sun Online*, August 29, 2006, http://www.thesun.co.uk/article/0,,2004580002-2006360057,00.html.

7. Martica Heaner, "Kick the Doughnut Habit, and Make Your Nutritionist Smile," *Nytimes.com*, May 3, 2005, http://www.nytimes.com/2005/05/03/health/nutrition/03cons.html?ei=5070&en=5375b161f8feeab2&ex=1134536400&adxnnl=1&adxnnlx=1134407142-VSspPtPXLeIFpuGygjG70g.

8. MacVean, "Krazy Kravings."

9. Tom Quinn, "Krispy Kreme Loses Its '03 Glaze," *The Oregonian*, July 5, 2004, http://www.oregonlive.com/news/oregonian/index.ssf?/base/news/1088855781264770.xml.

10. Bruce Horovitz, "Jumpin' Jelly! Doughnuts Dominate Dining Growth," *USA Today*, May 27, 2003, http://www.usatoday.com/money/industries/food/2003-05-27-doughnut-growth_x.htm.

11. Russell M. Nelson, "Our Sacred Duty to Honor Women," *Lightplanet.com*, 1999, http://www.lightplanet.com/mormons/conferences/99_apr/nelson_our.htm.

12. Bella English, "Dukin' Donuts," *Boston Globe*, June 27, 2003, http://www.azcentral.com/home/takeout/articles/0627donutwar27.html.

13. Laurib, "Donuts with Dads—A Great Success," *PTOtoday.com*, http://www.ptotoday.com/ubb/ultimatebb.php?ubb=get_topic;f=31;t=000002#000000.

14. Robert Tomsho, "A Doughnut Shop for Every 5,750 Residents," *Boston.com*, July 26, 2004, http://www.boston.com/news/local/rhode_island/articles/2004/07/26/a_doughnut_shop_for_every_5750_boston_residents/?rss_id=Boston.com%20/%20News.

15. "Southern Baptists Bring Gospel to New York," *Faith News Network*, February 16, 2004, www.faithnews.cc/fn3printit.cfm?sid=4037.

16. Heaner, "Kick the Doughnut Habit."

17. "Doughnut Hoax Means Death of a Dream Diet," *Sun Herald*, February 24, 2004, http://www.sunherald.com/mld/sunherald/8042692.htm.

18. Dana Milbank, "Operation Rumor Control Underway at Summit Site," *Washington Post*, June 24, 2004, A6.

19. Mintz, *Tasting Food, Tasting Freedom*, 18.

20. Mohegan Sun Casino, "Learn More about the Tribe," http://www.mohegansuncasinoe.com/about/the_tribe.jsp.

21. Mintz, *Tasting Food, Tasting Freedom*.

22. Ritzer, *The McDonaldization of Society*, 160–61.

23. Mintz, *Tasting Food, Tasting Freedom*, 112–15.

24. "Frequently Asked Questions," *Slowfood.com*, http://www.slowfood.com/eng/sf_stampa/sf_stampa_faq.lasso.

25. Jill MacBeath and Jen McCauley, "Dateline Atlantic Canada: Land of Lazy and Dumb," *King's Journalism Review*, October 2002, http://journalism.ukings.ns.ca.kjr/2002-2003/macbeath.htm.

26. Ryan Bigge, "The Donut Whole Story," *Chill Online*, August/September 2004, http://www.thebeerstore.ca/chill/Issue7/issue7-features-donut.html.

Chapter 2. Doughnut 101: A History of Doughnuts

1. "News of Food," *New York Times*, September 26, 1949, 28.

2. "Salvation Army Officer Cooks Doughnuts, As She Did in the War, for Fund Drive Here." *New York Times*, April 20, 1938, 10.

3. "Salvation Army Is a 'Hit' in Paris," *New York Times*, April 27, 1918, 8.

4. "Miss Booth Gets Ovation in France," *New York Times*, September 18, 1927, 3.

5. "Fried First Doughnuts for Soldiers Overseas," *New York Times* May 24, 1949, 6.

6. "Glory of Doughnut Revived at a Party," *New York Times*, May 14, 1936, 3.

7. "Y.M.C.A. Aided at St. Mihiel," *New York Times*, September 23, 1918, 4.

8. "M.P.'s Semaphore Turns the Trick," *Stars and Stripes*, August 2, 1918, 2.

9. "Glory of Doughnut Revived at a Party," 3.

10. Gabaccia, *We Are What We Eat*, 11.

11. Leslie Linthicum, "Indian Activist Urges Abstinence from Fry Bread," *Albuquerque Journal*, February 23, 2005, http://www.azstarnet.com/dailystar/news/62826.php.

12. Gabaccia, *We Are What We Eat*, 130.

13. Goldsmith, "Walking in Beauty at Sage Memorial Hospital," 29–30.

14. Irving, *A History of New York*, 149.

15. Steinberg, *The Donut Book*, 64–65.

16. Carter, *The Frugal Housewife*, 206.

17. For example, Murphy, "A History of the Doughnut."

18. Rose, *The Sensible Cook*, 78.

19. Brown, *"You Said a Mouthful."*

20. Jones, *American Food*, 91.

21. Julian Ralph, "The Origin of Buckwheat Cakes," *Brooklyn Eagle*, September 3, 1899, 15.

22. Melville, *Moby Dick*, 334.

23. Leslie, *Directions for Cookery*, 359.

24. "A Glimpse of an Old Dutch Town," *Harper's New Monthly Magazine*, March 1881, 533.

25. William Elliot Griffis, "The Dutch Influence in New England," *Harper's New Monthly Magazine*, January 1894, 218.

26. Leslie, *Seventy-five Receipts*; compare Hess and Hess, *The Taste of America*, 96.

27. Leslie, *Seventy-five Receipts*, 70; and Hess and Hess, *The Taste of America*, 100.

28. *The Cook Not Mad*.

29. Child, *The Frugal Housewife*.

30. Lincoln, *Mrs. Lincoln's Boston Cook Book*, 40.

31. Hess and Hess, *The Taste of America*, 57.

32. Gabaccia, *We Are What We Eat*, 57.

33. Howland, *The American Economical Housekeeper and Family Receipt Book*.

34. Allen, *The Housekeeper's Assistant*, 16–17.

35. Randolph, *The Virginia Housewife*, 12.

36. Wilcox, *Buckeye Cookery*, 76.

37. *Fullstandigaste Svensk-Americakansk Kokbok/Swedish-English Cookbook*, 140.

38. Fox, *The Blue Grass Cook Book*, 253.

39. Irving, "The Legend of Sleepy Hollow," p. 34, http://www.planetpdf.com/planetpdf/pdfs/free_ebooks/The_Legend_of_Sleepy_Hollow_NT.pdf; Thoreau, *Cape Cod*, 101.

40. Griffis, "The Dutch Influence in New England," 218; Eunice Fuller Barnard, "New York Still Has Its Dutch Roots," *New York Times* July 4, 1926, SM19.

41. William Elliot Griffis, *The Story of New Netherland*. Houghton Mifflin Company (Boston and New York, 1909). http://en.wikisource.org/wiki/The_Story_of_New_Netherland/Chapter_8.

42. Wilcox, *Buckeye Cookery*, 76.

43. Leslie, *Directions for Cookery*, 359.

44. "Housekeeping in Klondike," *Brooklyn Eagle*, September 19, 1900, 13.

45. "Doughnuts." *Dialect Notes*. New Haven, Conn.: American Dialect Society, 1895, 387.

46. "Doughnuts," *New York Times*, September 7, 1907, 8.

47. C. P. Benedict, "History of the Doughnut," letter, *New York Times*, December 30, 1916, 8.

48. L. H. Robbins, "Doughnut or Cruller?" *New York Times*, December 12, 1943, SM39.

49. J. L. A. Fowler, "The Cruller-Doughnut Question," letter, *New York Times*, December 6, 1913, 10.

50. Randolph, *The Virginia Housewife*, 12.

51. Glasse, *The Art of Cookery*, 138.

52. Leslie, *Seventy-five Receipts*, 70.

53. Leslie, *Directions for Cookery*, 359.

54. Ibid., 358.

55. Hearn, *La Cuisine Creole*, 139.

56. Ibid., 137.

57. Ibid., 138.

58. Aunt Babette, *"Aunt Babette's" Cook Book*, 177.

59. Ibid.

60. Grandma, "The Superior Doughnut," letter, *New York Times*, December 15, 1913, 8.

61. K. C., "Cruller and Doughnut Explained," letter, *New York Times*, December 7, 1913, C6.

62. "Hailed as Inventor of Hole in Doughnut," *New York Times*, January 31, 1937, 34.

63. Ibid.

64. Michael Grady, "The Doughnut: A Well-Rounded Tale," *East Valley Tribune*, June 22, 2004, http://www.eastvalleytribune.com/?sty=23512.

65. Denise Taylor, "Fresh Air Keep Your Krispys—We'll Take the Locally Raised Doughnuts," *Boston Globe*, August 14, 2003, 8; Murphy, "A History of the Doughnut," 1.

66. Steinberg, *The Donut Book*, 69; David A. Taylor, "Ring King," *Smithsonian Magazine*, March 1998, http://www.smithsonianmag.si.edu/smithsonian/issues89/mar98/object_mar98.html.

67. Jones, *American Food*, 91.

68. Ibid.; Steinberg, *The Donut Book*, 70.

69. "Doughnuts Delight Boys 'Over There,'" *Cleveland Advocate*, November 9, 1918, 7.

70. Irving, *A History of New York*, 148.

71. Thoreau, *Cape Cod*, 101.

72. Stowe, *Pogunac People*, 156.

73. S. Smith, *My Thirty Years Out of the Senate*, 33.

74. Stewart, *Letters of a Woman Homesteader*.

75. "Mr. James Lick," *New York Times,* October 2, 1876, 7.

76. Woods, *Foods of the Foreign-Born*, 42.

77. "Hanged on the Gallows," *New York Times*, April 17, 1886, 2.

78. Venice Cafeteria Menu, Los Angeles Public Library Menu Collection (1919), http://dbase1.lapl.org/dbtw-wpd/exec/dbtwpub.dll?AC=GET_RECORD&XC=http://dbase1.lapl.org/dbtw-wpd/exec/dbtwpub.dll&BU=http%3A%2F%2Fdbase1.lapl.org&TN=menus&SN=AUTO14259&SE=926&RN=5&MR=20&RF=web+tab+report+maya&DF=web+report+maya&RL=0&DL=0&NP=3&ID=&MF=&MQ=&TI=0.

79. "The Kitchen Cabinet," *Davis County Clipper*, September 2, 1921.

80. Advertisement, *New York Times*, March 16, 1932, 44.

81. Levenstein, *Paradox of Plenty*, 75.

82. Arthur J. Olsen, "U.S. Shows Food at Cologne Fair," *New York Times*, September 27, 1959, 9.

83. See, for example, Susman, *Culture as History*.

84. Ritzer, *The McDonaldization of Society*, 26–27.

85. Jakle and Sculle, *Fast Food*, 166.

86. Ibid., 197.

87. "Profiteer in Doughnuts," *New York Times*, September 18, 1921, 9.

88. "Thrills of Coney Island Doughboys' Delight," *New York Times*, October 5, 1919, 36.

89. "Adolph Levitt, 70, the Doughnut King," *New York Times*, October 30, 1953, 23; Steinberg, *The Donut Book*, 20.

90. Steinberg, *The Donut Book*, 22.

91. Advertisement, *New York Times*, April 30, 1920, 30.

92. Jefferson Moak, "The Frozen Sucker War: Good Humor v. Popsicle," *Prologue Magazine*, spring 2005, http://www.archives.gov/publications/prologue/2005/spring/popsicle-1.html.

93. Jessica R. Shely, "The Popsicle Turns 100," *Seattle Post-Intelligencer*, August 24, 2005, http://seattlepi.nwsource.com/food/237680_popsicle100.html.

94. Penfold, *The Social Life of Donuts*, 35.

95. "News of Food," 28.

96. Jakle and Sculle, *Fast Food*, 25.

97. Lowell K. Dyson, "American Cuisine in the 20th Century," *Food Review*, January 2000, 2–7.

98. Steinberg, *The Donut Book*, 35.

99. Ibid.

100. King, *How to Run a Successful Party*, 31.

101. Steinberg, *The Donut Book*, 34.

102. Rosenberg and Keener, *Time to Make the Donuts*, 106.

103. Ibid., 103.

104. Penfold, *The Social Life of Donuts*, 71–72.

105. Hurley, *Diners, Bowling Alleys, and Trailer Parks*, 5.

106. Jackson, *Crabgrass Frontier*, 263.

107. Ibid., 265.

108. Gentry Braswell, "Drive-thru at SV McDonald's Began Trend 30 Years Ago," *Sierra Vista Herald*, February 21, 2005, http://www.svherald.com/articles/2005/01/21/local_news/news2.prt.

109. Jackson, *Crabgrass Frontier*, 246.

110. Penfold, "'Eddie Shack Was No Tim Horton,'" 49, 53.

111. Jackson, *Crabgrass Frontier*, 238–41.

112. Jakle and Sculle, *Fast Food*, 38–39.

113. Ibid., 74–75.

114. Kazanjian and Joyner, *Making Dough*, xvi.

115. Sampson and Murdock Company, *The Boston Directory* for the year commencing July 1, 1925, http://bcd.lib.tufts.edu//view_text.jsp?urn=tufts:central:dca:UA069:UA069.005.DO.00005.

116. Rosenberg and Keener, *Time to Make the Donuts*, 92.

117. Jakle and Sculle, *Fast Food*, 73.

118. Rosenberg and Keener, *Time to Make the Donuts*, 97.

119. Ibid., 113–14.

120. Spudnuts, "Spudnut Shop," *Roadfood.com* post, February 22, 2004, http://www.roadfood.com/forums/topic.asp?TOPIC_ID=900&whichpage=1.

121. Rick Alm, "Kansas City Will Miss Its 'Doughnut King,'" *Kansas City Star*, November 12, 2005, http://www.kansascity.com/mld/kansascity/13147474.htm.

122. Olsen, "U.S. Shows Food at Cologne Fair," 9.

123. "Dairy Queen," *Wikipedia*, http://en.wikipedia.org/wiki/Dairy_Queen; Swift Current KFC, "History," http://www.eatkfc.com/history.html.

124. David's Dairy Queen, "Dairy Queen History," http://www.davidsdairyqueen.com/history.html.

125. Penfold, *The Social Life of Donuts*, 80.

126. Tim Hortons, "Media Kit," http://www.timhortons.com/en/news/media_kit.html.

127. Kazanjian and Joyner, *Making Dough*, xvi.

128. Ibid.

129. Jakle and Sculle, *Fast Food*, 200.

Chapter 3. Selling and Consuming the Doughnut

1. Monica Mercer, "Breakfast with AMERICA," *Express Newsline*, November 2, 2004, http://cities.expressindia.com/fullstory.php?newsid=105451.

2. King, *How to Run a Successful Party*, 30.

3. Bergman, *Ellis Island Oral History Project*, 34.

4. Dunn, *Ellis Island Oral History Project*, 26.

5. Jasinski, *Ellis Island Oral History Project*, 29.

6. Kevin Libin, "Holey War," *Canadian Business*, August 21, 2000, http://web.ebsco host.com/ehost/detail?vid=6&hid=108&sid=c48772a9-7617-47cc-aebe-96fc27eab171% 40sessionmgr101.

7. Ibid. The 2005 bankruptcy of Krispy Kreme's Canadian franchisee KremeCo shuttered some Canadian stores, but the chain continues with seven outlets, including its first Canadian store opened outside Toronto in 2001. See Sara Perkins, "KremeCo, Operator of Krispy Kreme Franchises in Canada, Up for Sale" *CBC News*, August 25, 2005, http://www.cbc.ca/cp/business/050610/b061096.html.

8. Scott Gardiner, "In Praise of Saint Timmy: Behind the Folksy Façade, Tim Hortons Is arguably Canada's Best-Oiled Marketing Machine." *Marketing Magazine*, August 21, 2000, http://proquest.umi.com/pqdweb?index=0&did=376058081&SrchMo de=1&sid=1&Fmt=3&VInst=PROD&VType=PQD&RQT=309&VName=PQD&TS=115 7487996&clientId=13225.

9. Penfold, *The Social Life of Donuts*.

10. Buist, *Tales from Under the Rim*, 33.

11. John Gray, "Treasure or Trash?" *Canadian Business*, June 7, 2004, http://www.wendys-invest.com/main/canadian_bus04.php.

12. Penfold, *The Social Life of Donuts*, 52.

13. Benjamin R. Barber, "Jihad vs. McWorld," *Atlantic Monthly*, March 1992, 53.

14. Penfold, *The Social Life of Donuts*, 53, 65.

15. Buist, *Tales from Under the Rim*, 61.

16. "Getting at the Hole Truth, Doughnuts: A Glazed Look," *Myst*, http://individual.utoronto.ca/myst/Gettingatthe HoleTruth.htm.

17. Gary Evans, "Highlights from the Book 'The 1995 Hamilton Almanac,'" *City of Hamilton*, www.hamilton.ca/visiting-here/about-hamilton/hamilton-almanac-highlights.asp.

18. Buist, *Tales from Under the Rim*, 35.

19. Robert Tomsho, "A Doughnut Shop for Every 5,750 Residents," *Boston.com*, July 26, 2004, http://www.boston.com/news/local/rhode_island/articles/2004/07/26/a _doughnut_shop_for_every_5750_boston_residents/?rss_id=Boston.com%20/%20 News.

20. Penfold, *The Social Life of Donuts*, 56.

21. Ibid.

22. Roy Blount Jr., "Southern Comfort," *New York Times*, September 8, 1996, SM67.

23. Edward Keenan, "Au Viex Cruller," *The Eye*, December 5, 2002, http://www/eye.net/eye/issue_12.05.02/city/donuts.html.

24. Buist, *Tales from Under the Rim*, 35.

25. Keenan, "Au Viex Cruller."

26. Penfold, *The Social Life of Donuts*, 58.

27. Joe Follick, "Gov. Bush Defends His Record of Tax Cuts," *Gainesville.com,* http://www.gainesville.com/apps/pbcs.dll/article?AID=/20051204/LOCAL/212040319.

28. Buist, *Tales from Under the Rim*, 117.

29. Penfold, *The Social Life of Donuts*, 54.

30. Ibid., 52.

31. Ibid., 60.

32. "Krispy Kreme Doughnuts History," *Krispy Kreme Incorporated*, http://www.krispykreme.com/presskit.pdf.

33. Connie, "Krispy Kreme Gets Burnt," *Philadelphia Daily News,* Girlfriends' Locker Room post, May 7, 2004, http://www.pnionline.com/dnblog/fit/archives/000444.html.

34. Buist, *Tales from Under the Rim*, 197.

35. For example, Breed, "The Rise and Fall of Krispy Kreme," *Laredo Morning Times,* January 23, 2005, 30.

36. Kazanjian and Joyner, *Making Dough*, xiv.

37. Mark Maremont and Rick Brooks, "Once-Hot Krispy Kreme Ousts Its CEO Amid Accounting Woes," *Wall Street Journal*, January 19, 2005, A1.

38. Kazanjian and Joyner, *Making Dough*, 7.

39. Ibid., 25.

40. Kim Severson, "The Hole Truth: Can America Build a Better Doughnut? Does It Need To?" *San Francisco Chronicle*, March 17, 2004, http://sfgate.com/cgi-bin/article.cgi?f=/chronicle/archive/2004/03/17/FDGDM5J57Q1.DTL; Jakle and Sculle, *Fast Food*, 199.

41. Criddle, *Bamboo and Butterflies*, 32.

42. Davis, *Cambodian Doughnut Dreams*.

43. Debbie Gardiner, "Donuts Anyone?" *AsianWeek.com*, June 22, 2000, http://www.asianweek.com/2000_06_22/biz1_cambodiandonutbiz.html.

44. Ibid.

45. Ibid.

46. Davis, *Cambodian Doughnut Dreams*.

47. Kazanjian and Joyner, *Making Dough*, viii.

48. Karen Bartlett, "Rise and Fall of a Doughnut," *New Statesman*, December 13, 2004, 51, http://www.newstatesman.com/200412130034.

49. Denise Taylor, "Fresh Air Keep Your Krispys—We'll Take the Locally Raised Doughnuts," *Boston Globe,* August 14, 2003, 8.

50. Amy McFall Prince, "New Spin on Doughnuts." *Franchising.cn*, February 26, 2004, http://chainstore.cn/news/9/4646.html.

51. Bonnie Brewer Cavanaugh, "Going Nuts Over Doughnuts," *Nations' Restaurant News*, January 2005, http://www.nrn.com/story.cfm?ID=3128302277&SEC=Dessert%20T.html.

52. Taylor, "Fresh Air Keep Your Krispys," 8.

53. Kazanjian and Joyner, *Making Dough*, 199.

54. Cavanaugh, "Going Nuts Over Doughnuts"; "Customers Say Hotties Is Better Than Other Donut Shops," *Bizjournals*, November 19, 2002, http://bizjournals.bison.com/press/pr11-19-02hotties.html.

55. Severson, "The Hole Truth."

56. Amy McFall Prince, "New Spin on Doughnuts." *Franchising.cn*, February 26, 2004, http://chainstore.cn/news/9/4646.html.

57. Russell E. DiCarlo, "Intuitively Perceiving the Human Energy Field," *Health World Online*, December 6, 2002, http://www.healthy.net/scr/interview.asp?id=210.

58. David Spates, "Sometimes You Need a Doughnut," *Crossville Chronicle*, July 29, 2003, http://www.crossville-chronicle.com/Chronicle/Opinion/davedoughnut.html.

59. Blount, "Southern Comfort," SM67.

60. Denise Barnes, "Long Lines Greet Doughnut Shop," *Washington Times*, August 25, 2004, http://nl.newsbank.com/nl-search/we/Archives?p_product=WT&p_theme=wt&p_action=search&p_maxdocs=200&p_text_search-0=Long%20AND%20lines%20AND%20greet%20AND%20doughnut%20AND%20shop&s_dispstring=Long%20lines%20greet%20doughnut%20shop%20AND%20date(08/25/2004%20to%2008/25/2004)&p_field_date-0=YMD_date&p_params_date-0=date:B,E&p_text_date-0=08/25/2004%20to%2008/25/2004)&p_perpage=10&p_sort=YMD_date:D&xcal_useweights=no.

61. Lynn Collier, "New Yorker Hopes for Krispy Craze," *View*, January 27, 1998, http://www.viewnews.com/1998/VIEW-Jan-27-Tue-1998/NWest/6806606.html.

62. Tony Adams, "Doughnut Wars," *Ledger-Enquirer*, June 14, 2004, www.ledger-enquirer.com/mld/enquirer/8916646.htm.

63. Charles Pollen Adams, "Mother's Doughnuts," *Brooklyn Eagle*, June 28, 1885, 2.

64. Quoted in Sally L. Steinberg, "How Doughnuts Won America," *New York Times*, May 6, 1981, C4.

65. Corson, *Miss Corson's Practical American Cookery*, 13.

66. "Pies and Doughnuts for Men Up Front," *Stars and Stripes*, March 29, 1918, 3.

67. "Salvation Army Is a 'Hit' in Paris," *New York Times*, April 27, 1918, 8.

68. L. H. Robbins, "Doughnut or Cruller?" *New York Times*, December 12, 1943, SM39.

69. For example, "Comment: The Next Krispy Kreme," *danieldrezner.com*, http://www.danieldrezner.com/mt/mt-comments.cgi?entry_id=1781; Mary MacVean, "Krazy Kravings," *Salon*, March 10, 2000, http://dir.salon.com/travel/food/feature/2000/03/10/kreme/index.html.

70. K. D. Hobgood, "Hayride Heyday," *Neonbridge,* http://www.neonbridge.com/Articles/2000-2002/Hayride%20Heyday.htm.

71. Buist, *Tales from Under the Rim,* 62, 205.

72. Ibid., 58.

73. Ibid., 115, 205.

74. Rosenberg and Keener, *Time to Make the Donuts,* 221.

75. Ira Berkow, "The 'Seinfeld' Steinbrenner: The Head Yankee, Deconstructed," *New York Times,* March 28, 1996, C1.

76. Home page, *Dreesen's Famous Donuts,* http://www.dreesens.com.

77. Barnes, "Long Lines Greet Doughnut Shop."

78. Elissa Gootman, "Island a Battleground in the Doughnut War," *New York Times,* June 10, 2001, L12.

79. Akilah Johnson, "'Hot Light' Greets Eager Fans at New Boca Raton, Fla. Krispy Kreme," *Knight Ridder Tribune Business News,* June 22, 2004, 1.

80. Chelsi Moy, "'Raging Enthusiasm' Greets Montana's First Krispy Kreme," *Billings Gazette* July 28, 2004, B3.

81. Ryan Bigge, "The Donut Whole Story," *Chill Online,* August/September 2004, http://www.thebeerstore.ca/chill/Issue7/issue7-features-donut.html.

82. "Krispy Kreme Comes to Life in Medford, Massachusetts," *Tacquitos.net,* http://www.taquitos.net/snacks.php?page_code=13.

83. "Living History: Krispy Kreme Finally Opens in Boston." *Tacquitos.net,* http://www.taquitos.net/snacks.php?page_code=76.

84. Kazanjian and Joyner, *Making Dough,* 21–22.

85. Mark Maremont and Rick Brooks, "Sticky Situation: Ovens Are Cooling at Krispy Kreme as Woes Multiply; Lower Profit, Slower Growth, Informal SEC Probe Beset a Cultural Phenomenon; for Sale at Truck Stops Now," *Wall Street Journal,* September 3, 2004, A1.

86. "Minneapolis Declares War on Krispy Kreme," *Metafilter,* http://www.metafilter.com/comments.mefi/16854.

87. "Upper Crust," *Bakery and Snacks.com,* http://bakeryandsnacks.com/news/news-NG.asp?n=14024-upper-crust.

88. Dick Larkin, "How to Be a Doughnut (Not a-hole)," *Yellow Pages Commando,* http://ypcommando.com/articles/How%20to%20be%20a%20Doughnut.htm.

89. Sara Bir, "Do-Nut Believe the Hype," *Metroactive.com,* February 20, 2003, http://www.metroactive.com/papers/sonoma/02.20.03/donuts-0308.html.

90. Kazanjian and Joyner, *Making Dough,* 2.

91. Thomas Scoville, "Holy Pastry," *Salon.com,* March 10, 2000, http://www.salon.com/travel/food/feature/2000/03/10/bardo/index.html.

92. Cavanaugh, "Going Nuts Over Doughnuts."

93. *Food Crazy,* "Donut Crazy," February 18, 2004, Food Channel.

94. Colleen Van Tassell, "Star Quality," *New Haven Advocate,* January 29, 2004, http://www.newhavenadvocate.com/gbase/Dining/content?oid=oid:51738.

95. Rosenberg and Keener, *Time to Make the Donuts*, 119.

96. Paula Span, "Teens Are, Like, So Next Week," *Washington Post*, June 17, 1999, http://www.youthintelligence.com/company/yiarticle.asp?yiArticleID=6.

97. "Brand Mot," *Brand Strategy*, September 2004, 10–11.

98. Andy Serwer, "A Hole in Krispy Kreme's Story," *Fortune*, June 12, 2004, http://money.cnn.com/magazines/fortune/fortune_archive/2004/06/14/372629/index.htm.

99. Taylor, "Fresh Air Keep Your Krispys," 8.

100. For example, Krauss, "Police Officers (Quick, Which Food Comes to Mind?)," *New York Times*, September 22, 1996, E2.

101. Lorena Johnson, "Mmm, Doughnuts," *Calgary Sun*, http://www.calgarysun.com/cgi-bin/printable.cgi?article=82950.

102. Melanie D. Hayes, "Doughnut Shop a Lifelong Habit for Soden," *The Herald Bulletin.com*, http://www.theheraldbulletin.com/story.asp?id=5430.

103. Bonnie Friedman, "Fireworks on Fourth," *Jersey Journal*, July 1, 2005, 3.

104. Matthew Egan, "Live at Live 8 Philly—Impressions from the Ground," *Blogcritics.org*, http://blogcritics.org/archives/2005/07/03/124905.php.

105. Adam Bulger, "Bad Cop, No Donut," *Hartford Advocate*, June 23, 2005, http://www.hartfordadvocate.com/gbase/News/content?oid=oid:116568.

106. John Kidman, "There'll Be No Freebie Doughnuts on My Beat, Chief Orders," *Sydney Morning Herald*, April 10, 2005, http://www.smh.com.au/news/National/Police-suffer-doughnut-ban/2005/04/09/1112997229759.html.

107. Krauss, "Police Officers," E2.

108. "Operation Wellness," *Ball State Alumnus Magazine*, July 2005, http://www.bsu.edu/alumni/july05/facultyspot/.

109. Krauss, "Police Officers," E2.

110. Larry Higgs, "For Pinup Police Officers, Pride Mightier Than Muscle," *Courier News Online*, http://www.c-n.com/apps/pbcs.dll/article?AID=/20050713/NEWS/507130329.

111. "Stolen Krispy Kreme Truck Recovered; Cops 'Confiscate' Donuts," *American International Automobile Dealers Association*, December 3, 2004, http://www.aiada.org/article.asp?id=29009.

112. Rudy Cheeks, "Ask Dr. Lovemonkey," *Boston Phoenix*, November 30, 2000, http://www.bostonphoenix.com/archive/lovemonkey/00/11/30/lovemonkey.html.

113. Krauss, "Police Officers," E2.

114. Johnson, "Mmm, Doughnuts."

115. Gootman, "Island a Battleground in the Doughnut War," L12.

116. Laura Leedy, "Don't Call Me Palcho: The Man behind the Donuts Isn't So Sweet on College Students." *The CyBurr*, Fall 1998, http://www.burr.kent.edu/archives/1998/fall/palcho.html.

117. Jolene Bussiere, "Response to Development and the Youth Culture Article," *ENC 1102 Blog*, http://writingblog.org/jolenesblog.

118. Chapman and Maclean, "'Junk Food' and 'Healthy Food,'" 108–13.

119. Lang, *Tomorrow Is Beautiful*, 303.

120. Compare Kear, "If You've Seen One You've Seen Them All?"

121. Buist, *Tales from Under the Rim*, 60.

122. Ibid., 203.

123. Ibid., 170.

124. Michelle Prather, "Holey War," *Entrepreneur Magazine*, February 2000, http://www.Entrepreneur.com/article/0,,4621,232659,00.html.

125. For example, Buist, *Tales from Under the Rim*, 60.

126. Laura Weiss, "Bruegger's: Bagel Chain Seeks to Raise More Dough by Serving Different Dayparts," *Nation's Restaurant News*, January 31, 2005, 38, 40.

127. William C. Symonds, David Kiley, and Stanley Holmes, "A Java Jolt for Dunkin' Donuts," *Business Week Online*, December 20, 2004, http://www.businessweek.com/magazine/content/04_51/b3913090.htm.

128. Jesse Noyes, "Java Gibe: Ads Mock Starbucks," *Boston Herald.com*, September 13, 2006, http://business.bostonherald.com/businessNews/view.bg?articleid=157269.

129. "Starbucks Rolls 260-Unit Doughnut Test in Seattle," *Nation's Restaurant News*, January 24, 2005, http://www.findarticles.com/p/articles/mi_m3190/is_6_39/ai_n9523216.

130. Seacyn, "Report: Starbucks to Sell Top Pot 'Hand Forged' Donuts in at Least Some Stores," *Starbucks Gossip*, http://starbucksgossip.typepad.com/_/2005/01/report_starbuck.html.

131. Klein, *No Logo*, 24.

132. Starbucks, *Beyond the Cup: Corporate Social Responsibility Fiscal 2005 Annual Report,* http://www.starbucks.com/aboutus/FY05_CSR_Total.pdf.

133. "Restaurants and Bars: Long-Term Contribution Trends," *Opensecrets.org,* http://www.opensecrets.org/industries/indus.asp?Ind=G2900; Derrick Z. Jackson, "Trash Food Makers Fatten GOP Coffers," *Boston Globe.com*, March, 12, 2004, http://www.boston.com/news/globe/editorial_opinion/oped/articles/2004/03/12/trash_food_makers_fatten_gop_coffers/.

134. D. Z. Jackson, "Trash Food Makers Fatten GOP Coffers."

135. Ibid.

136. Bill Lambrecht, "Democrats Struggle to Change Perceptions in GOP Strongholds," *St. Louis Post-Dispatch*, August 13, 2005, B1.

137. Buist, *Tales from Under the Rim*, 195.

138. Kazanjian and Joyner, *Making Dough*, 132.

139. Ibid., 133.

140. I-chun Che, "The Donut Wheel in Cupertino Is the Quintessential Community Hangout," *Cupertino Courier,* February 11, 2004, http://www.community-newspapers.com/archives/cupertinocourier/20040211/cu-cover1.shtml.

141. Russell Mahakian, "O's in the O," *San Francisco Bay Guardian*, August 10, 2004, http://www.sfbg.com/38/45/x_biznews.html.

142. Ian Stewart, "Donut Chow Fun," *Prism Online*, http://www.journalism.sfsu.edu/www/pubs/prism/mar95/donu.htm..

143. Paul Fredericks, "Emmett Woman Creates a Donut Shop Memorial," *KBCI 2*, June 8, 2004, http://www.kbcitv.com/x54094.xml.

144. Donovan Slack, "Confection Contention," *Boston.com*, October 9, 2004, http://nl.newsbank.com/nl-search/we/Archives?p_product=BG&p_theme=bg&p_action=search&p_maxdocs=200&p_text_search-0=Confection%20AND%20contention&s_dispstring=Confection%20contention%20AND%20date(10/9/2004%20to%2010/9/2004)&p_field_date-0=YMD_date&p_params_date-0=date:B,E&p_text_date-0=10/9/2004%20to%2010/9/2004)&p_perpage=10&p_sort=YMD_date:D&xcal_useweights=no.

145. Ibid.

146. Tomsho, "A Doughnut Shop for Every 5,750 Residents."

147. Devlin Smith, "In the Fast Lane," *Entrepreneur.com*, August 26, 2002, http://www.entrepreneur.com/article/0,4621,302649,00.html.

148. Buist, *Tales from Under the Rim*, 50.

149. Ibid., 51.

150. Charity Vogel, "Hunger for Doughnuts Insatiable," *Buffalo News Online*, February 6, 2005, http://nl.newsbank.com/nl-search/we/Archives?p_product=BN&p_theme=bn&p_action=search&p_maxdocs=200&p_field_label-0=Author&p_text_label-0=Charity%20Vogel&s_dispstring=Hunger%20for%20doughnuts%20insatiable%20AND%20source(Charity%20Vogel)&p_field_date-0=YMD_date&p_params_date-0=date:B,E&p_text_date-0=2005&p_field_advanced-0=&p_text_advanced-0=(%22Hunger%20for%20doughnuts%20insatiable%22)&p_perpage=10&p_sort=YMD_date:D&xcal_useweights=no.

151. Buist, *Tales from Under the Rim*, 51.

152. Smith, "In the Fast Lane."

153. Buist, *Tales from Under the Rim*, 201.

154. Amy McFall Prince, "New Spin on Doughnuts." *Franchising.cn*, February 26, 2004, http://chainstore.cn/news/9/4646.html.

155. T. Adams, "Doughnut Wars."

156. Taylor, "Fresh Air Keep Your Krispys," 8.

157. Brian Louis, "Krispy Kreme to Open Western Canadian Store," *Winston-Salem Journal*, September 4, 2003.

158. Andrews, "Krispy Kreme Bakes Up a Big Expansion Plan," *Indianapolis Business Journal*, January 31, 1994, 5A.

159. Buist, *Tales from Under the Rim*, 59.

160. "Doughnuts Take Over in Africa," *New Pittsburgh Courier*, October 14, 1961, 4.

Chapter 4. Doughnut Morals

1. Compare Horowitz, *The Morality of Spending*.

2. De Tocqueville, *Democracy in America*, 536.

3. Thoreau, *Walden*.

4. Veblen, *The Theory of the Leisure Class*.

5. Bruce Horovitz, "Jumpin' Jelly! Doughnuts Dominate Dining Growth," *USA Today*, May 27, 2003, http://www.usatoday.com/money/industries/food/2003-05-27-doughnut-growth_x.htm.

6. "Jim Schoenfeld," *Hockey Draft Central*, http://hockeydraftcentral.com/1972 /72005.html.

7. Alcott, *The Young Housekeeper*, 113.

8. "Late Southern News," *New York Times*, December 1, 1864, 2.

9. Julian Ralph, "The Origin of Buckwheat Cakes," *Brooklyn Eagle*, September 3, 1899, 15.

10. "The Fear of Fat." *New York Times*, March 15, 1880, 8.

11. Michael Williams, "We All Eat Too Much," *New York Times*, May 25, 1907, BR329.

12. "Says Pupils Receive Scanty Breakfasts," *New York Times*, June 1, 1929, 20.

13. Levenstein, *Paradox of Plenty*, 15.

14. Crum, *Beauty and Health*.

15. "War and Spring Vie for Influence at Show for 30,000 Beauty Shop Proprietors," *New York Times*, March 19, 1941, 23.

16. Crum, *Beauty and Health*, 79.

17. Ibid., 76.

18. Brown, *"You Said a Mouthful,"* 23.

19. Crum, *Beauty and Health*, 80; Paul D. Paddock, "Dollars from Doughnuts," *Nation's Business*, May 1941, 88–89.

20. "Superflour," *New York Times*, January 12, 1941, E8.

21. Levenstein, *Paradox of Plenty*, 75.

22. Jane Nickerson, "New Doughnut Recipe Adds Food Value to an Old Standby," *New York Times*, September 29, 1954, 26.

23. Sorensen, *Ellis Island Oral History Project*.

24. Levenstein, *Paradox of Plenty*, 59.

25. "Put Milk First in Food Values," *New York Times*, January 3, 1927, 36.

26. Levenstein, *Paradox of Plenty*, 59.

27. "Dairy Experts Map Study of Nutrition," *New York Times*, June 23, 1934, 13.

28. "Dairy Organizations Plan a Sales Drive," *New York Times*, September 19, 1938, 33.

29. "Advertising News and Notes," *New York Times*, September 17, 1940, 40.

30. George Gallup, "Use of Milk by the Average U.S. Family Is below Health Diet," *New York Times*, December 6, 1941, 13.

31. "Dairy Sales Drive Started," *New York Times*, March 25, 1953, 27.

32. American Dairy Association, *Grins and Gripes of the Grocer*.

33. Joan Cook, "Today's Slender American Woman Is Frequently Size 12 Going on 10," *New York Times*, February 15, 1960, 30.

34. Nan Ickeringill, "Fancy Foods to Vie with Low-Calorie Diet Products," *New York Times*, December 31, 1960, 9.

35. Nagle, "Diet Foods Gaining as Customers Lose," 1.

36. William Borders, "New Diet Decried by Nutritionists," *New York Times*, July 7, 1965, 16; William Borders, "Drinking Man's Diet—Is It All Wet?" *New York Times*, July 11, 1965, E6.

37. Borders, "New Diet Decried by Nutritionists," 16.

38. Amy McFall Prince, "New Spin on Doughnuts." *Franchising.cn*, February 26, 2004, http://chainstore.cn/news/9/4646.html.

39. Paul Nowell, "Is the Glaze Off Krispy Kreme?" *CBS News*, May 13, 2004, www.cbsnews.com/stories/2004/05/13/national/main617329.shtml.

40. "Krispy Kreme Hit by Atkins Craze," *BBC News*, May 7, 2004, http://news.bbc.co.uk/go/pr/fr/-/1/hi/business/3694371.stm.

41. "Krispy Kreme to Make Low-carb Doughnuts," *Providence Journal*, May 28, 2004, http://www.projo.com/cgi-bin/include.pl/blogs/shenews/archives/week107.htm.

42. Nowell, "Is the Glaze Off Krispy Kreme?"

43. "Wendy's Reports Strong April Sales," *Business First of Columbus*, May 3, 2004, http://columbus.bizjournals.com/columbus/stories/2004/05/03/daily1.html.

44. "LaMar's Fends Off Low-Carb Fad," *Denver Business Journal*, October 6, 2004, http://denver.bizjournals.com/denver/stories/2004/10/04/daily34.html.

45. Theresa Johnson, "Krispy Kreme Gets Burnt," *Philadelphia Daily News,* Girlfriends' Locker Room, May 7, 2004, http://www.pnionline.com/dnblog/fit/archives/000444.html.

46. J. Scott Wilson, "A Boy and His Doughnut," *KIROTV.com*, May 17, 2004, http://kirotv.com/print/3293029/detail.html.

47. Horovitz, "Jumpin' Jelly!"

48. "The Donut Franchise: Historically a Sweet Deal." *Franchising.com*, http://www.franchising.com/article.php?id=96.

49. Ibid.

50. Kathleen McLaughlin, "Low-Carb Fad Takes a Bite Out of Snack Food Profits," *North Andover Eagle Tribune*, May 30, 2004, http://www.eagletribune.com/news/stories/20040530/BU_002.htm.

51. Ibid.

52. Nowell, "Is the Glaze Off Krispy Kreme?"

53. John Schmeltzer, "Atkins Goes Belly Up as Diet Fad Thins Out." *Chicago Tribune.com*, http://pqasb.pqarchiver.com/chicagotribune/access/876192821.html?FMT=FT&FMTS=FT&date=Aug+2%2C+2005&author=John+Schmeltzer%2C+Tribune+staff+reporter&pub=Chicago+Tribune&desc=Atkins+goes+belly-up+as+diet+fad+thins+out+%3B+Competition%2C+backlash+bring+on+Chapter+11.

54. David Wellman, "Low Carb," *Frozen Food Age,* http://frozenfoodage.com/printpage.asp?article_id=1149.

55. Jimmy Moore, "The Worst Possible Food You Could Eat on Low-Carb," *Commonvoice.com,* http://www.commonvoice.com/article.asp?colid=2163.

56. Schmeltzer, "Atkins Goes Belly Up."

57. Trager, *The Food Chronology,* 113.

58. Gabaccia, *We Are What We Eat,* 3.

59. Bernstein and Carstensen, "Rising to the Occasion," 170.

60. Trager, *The Food Chronology,* 451.

61. For example, "Pay Rise Frees Bagels," *New York Times,* June 8, 1948, 27; "Bagels, Absent 8 Weeks, Back on Sale Tomorrow," *New York Times,* February 8, 1952, 24.

62. "Bagels, Absent 8 Weeks, Back on Sale Tomorrow," 24.

63. June Owen, "Food News: Never Boil the Bagels," May 4, 1960, 53.

64. Beatrice Freeman and Ira Henry Freeman, "About: Bagels," *New York Times,* May 22, 1960, SM93–94.

65. Bernstein and Carstensen, "Rising to the Occasion," 171–72.

66. Gabaccia, *We Are What We Eat,* 4; Bernstein and Carstensen, "Rising to the Occasion," 173.

67. "A Campaign to Roll Out the Bagel," *New York Times,* November 4, 1965, 69.

68. Bernstein and Carstensen, "Rising to the Occasion," 174.

69. Gabaccia, *We Are What We Eat,* 4.

70. Bryan Curtis, "Dunkin' Donuts: A More Perfect Pastry," *Slate,* March 2, 2005, http://slate.msn.com/toolbar.aspx?/action=print&id=2114265.

71. For example, William Safire, "Bagels vs. Doughnuts," *New York Times,* October 25, 1999, A31.

72. Laura Weiss, "Bruegger's: Bagel Chain Seeks to Raise More Dough by Serving Different Dayparts," *Nation's Restaurant News,* January 31, 2005, 38.

73. "A Bagel or a Donut?" *Health and Nutrition Letter,* July 2003, http://healthletter.tufts.edu/issues/2003-07/bagel_or_donut.html.

74. Karen Collins, "Think Muffins and Bagels Are Healthy? Think Again." *msnbc.com,* October 22, 2005, http://www.msnbc.com/id/6307384/print/1/displaymode/1098/.

75. Charity Vogel, "Hunger for Doughnuts Insatiable," *Buffalo News Online,* February 6, 2005, http://nl.newsbank.com/nl-search/we/Archives?p_product=BN&p_theme=bn&p_action=search&p_maxdocs=200&p_field_label-0=Author&p_text_label-0=Charity%20Vogel&s_dispstring=Hunger%20for%20doughnuts%20insatiable%20AND%20source(Charity%20Vogel)&p_field_date-0=YMD_date&p_params_date-0=date:B,E&p_text_date-0=2005&p_field_advanced-0=&p_text_advanced-0=(%22Hunger%20for%20doughnuts%20insatiable%22)&p_perpage=10&p_sort=YMD_date:D&xcal_useweights=no.

76. Weiss, "Bruegger's," 40.

77. Safire, "Bagels vs. Doughnuts," A31.

78. "Airport Food Review," *Physicians Committee for Responsible Medicine*, Winter 2003, http://www.pcrm.org/health/reports/airport_food_review.html.

79. "America's Fattest Cities 2005," *Men's Fitness*, http://www.mensfitness.com/rankings/304.

80. Natasha Chin, "America's Fattest and Fittest Cities: Fort Worth," *Men's Fitness*, http://www.mensfitness.com/rankings/269.

81. Ellen Goodman, "The Vehicle Leading to Obesity," *Boston Globe*, February 2, 2005, www.boston.com/news/globe/editorial_opinion/oped/articles/2004/02/08/the_vehicle_leading_to _obesity/.

82. Neil Rogers, "And the Fattest City Is . . . ," *The Neil Rogers Show*, http://news.neilrogers.com/news/articles/2005011003.html.

83. *The Simpsons*, "Sweets and Sour Marge."

84. "Texas Law Would Tax Junk Food for Schools," *Bignewsnetwork.com*, http://feeds.bignewsnetwork.com/?sid=bc33b42d6635e9a4.

85. Diane Rado, "Governor Again Takes on School Junk Food," *Chicago Tribune*, November 29, 2005, http://www.chicagotribune.com/news/local/chi-0511290027nov29,1,1916384.story.

86. "2003 School Lunch Report Card," *Physicians Committee for Responsible Medicine*, August 2003, http://www.healthyschoollunches.org/reports/report2003_card.html.

87. "Schwarzenegger Signs High School Soda Ban," *AMonline.com*, September 16, 2005, www.amonline.com/article/printer.jsp?id=14525.

88. Neal Peirce, "Time to Get Tough on Soda Pop," *Seattle Times*, September 12, 2005, http://seattletimes.nwsource.com/html/opinion/2002488368_peirce12.html.

89. Ibid.

90. Derrick Z. Jackson, "Why Obesity is Winning," *The Boston Globe*, August 19, 2005, http://www.boston.com/news/globe/editorial_opinion/oped/articles/2005/08/19/why_obesity_is_winning/.

91. Tom Harkin, "Providing Healthier Alternatives at School," Senator Tom Harkin home page, June 2, 2004, http://harkin.senate.gov/column.cfm?id=224619.

92. Brigid Schulte, "More Nutritious, Less Delicious," *Washington Post*, June 27, 2002, B1.

93. Ibid.

94. Josie Huang, "Snack Rule May Choke Fundraising," *Portland Press Herald*, September 18, 2005, http://pressherald.maintoday.com/news/state/150918snack.shtml.

95. Mark Tatge, "Get Ready for the Twinky Tax," *MSNBC.com*, February 3, 2004, http://msnbc.msn.com/id/4131830/.

96. Parija Bhatnager, "Burgers, Fries, and Fast-Food Tax to Go?" *CNN Money*, http://money.cnn.com/2005/05/09/news/economy/fastfood_tax/index.htm.

97. Tatge, "Get Ready for the Twinkie Tax."

98. Margo MacDonald, "Doughnuts a Zero for Nation's Health," *Edinburgh Evening*

News, October 1, 2003, http://business.scotsman.com/topics.cfm?tid=751&id=1086 692003.

99. "Doughnut-Shaped Peaches Hit Shops," *BBC News,* July 28, 2005, http://news. bbc.co.uk/go/pr/fr/-/2/hi/uk_news/4721913.stm.

100. Susan Deutschle, "Programs Meet Resistance as Retailers Want to Know More," *Business First of Columbus,* May 24, 2002, http://sanjose.bizjournals.com/ sanjose/stories/2002/05/27/focus4.html.

101. Jonathan Rowe and Gary Ruskin, "Bush in Bed with the Global Obesity Lobby," *Organic Consumers Association,* http://www.organicconsumers.org/corp/ obesity 012704.cfm; Radley Balko, "Are You Responsible for Your Own Weight?" *Time,* June 7, 2004, 113.

102. Rowe and Ruskin, "Bush in Bed with the Global Obesity Lobby."

103. "What Is the Center for Consumer Freedom?" *consumerfreedom.com,* http:// www.consumerfreedom.com/about.cfm.

104. "Center for Consumer Freedom," *Wikipedia,* http://en.wikipedia.org/wiki/ Center_for_Consumer_Freedom; Richard B. Berman to Ms. Barbara Trach, letter, *Center for Media and Democracy,* http://www.prwatch.org/documents/berman/ berman600k.pdf.

105. Jennifer Harper, "The Seductive Quality of Food Is All in the Brain," *Washington Times,* June 15, 2003, http://washingtontimes.com/national/20030615-121437-1320r.htm.

106. Christen Brownlee, "Food Fix," *Science News Online,* September 3, 2005, http://www.sciencenews.org/articles/20050903/bob10.asp.

107. Bruce Bartlett, "The Big Food Tax," *National Review Online,* April 3, 2002, http://www.nationalreview.com/nrof_bartlett/bartlett040302.asp.

108. Balko, "Are You Responsible for Your Own Weight?" 113.

109. Levy, Levy, Le Pen, and Basdevant, "The Economic Cost of Obesity."

110. Patricia Wells, "Putting Nutrition into Hispanic Diets," *New York Times,* November 2, 1977, 54.

111. "Bush Blames 'Too Many Doughnuts' for Weight Gain," *New Zealand Herald,* December 13, 2004, http://www.nzherald.co.nz/topic/story.cfm?c_id=500829&ObjectID=9002891.

112. "Junk Food Ads Spur Kids' Obesity," *Preventdisease.com,* July 21, 2005, http:// preventdisease.com/news/articles/072105_junk_food_obesity.shtml.

113. Vogel, "Hunger for Doughnuts Insatiable."

114. MacDonald, "Doughnuts a Zero for Nation's Health."

115. Alex Massie, "US Doughnut Chains Target Britons in the Battle of the Bulge," *Business.scotsman.com,* October 19, 2003, http://business.scotsman.com/topics.cfm? tid=751&id=1155482003.

116. Todd Buchholz, "The Workplace's Role In Our Expanding Waistlines," *NBR. com,* http://www.nightlybusiness.org/transcript/2005/transcript071905.html.

117. Thuy-Doan Le, "Fit to Do Business," *Sacramento Bee*, http://www.apria.com/common/aw_cmp_printNews/1,2762,356684,00.html.

118. "Councilor Wants to Ban Doughnuts in City Hall," *Thebostonchannel.com*, May 23, 2005, http://www.thebostonchannel.com/print/4521684/detail.html.

119. Daneesha R. Davis, "Hugs, Mugs, and Doughnuts," *Winchester Star*, January 13, 2005, http://www.winchesterstar.com/TheWinchesterStar/050113/Area_hugs.asp.

120. Megan Means, "Doughnuts Lure Volunteers," *Columbia Daily Tribune*, October 13, 2004, http://www.columbiatribune.com/2004/Oct/20041013News004.asp.

121. Janet Sugameli, "Dads Broaden Role at School," *Detnews.com*, February 7, 2005, http://www.detnews.com/2005/schools/0502/07/B04-81345.htm.

122. Susan Cairo, "Dads Get Doughnuts and Bonding Time," *Venicegondolier.com*, September 27, 2006, http://www.venicegondolier.com/NewsArchive3/092706/tp3vn6.htm.

123. Sarah V. Sandro, "Doughnuts for Dads Hits Upper Providence," *Spring-Ford Reporter*, September 30, 2004, http://www.zwire.com/site/news.cfm?newsid=130418 61&BRD=1306&PAG=461&dept_id=187825&rfi=8.

124. Nirvi Shah, "Doughnuts-for-A's Weighs Heavily on School Board," *PalmBeachPost.com*, August 25, 2004, http://www.lap-band-surgery.org/obesity.cfm/48886925/Krispy-Kreme-confronts-childhood-obesity-problem-by-offering-free-donuts-to-kids-who-do-well-in-school/index.html.

125. Jabari Asim, "You Can't Sugarcoat This School Promotion," *News-Press.com*, http://vh10066.v1.moc.gbahn.net/apps/pbcs.dll/article?AID=/20040910/OPINION/409100350/1015.

126. Miss Zoot, "Honor Roll," *Miss Zoot Blog*, post August 25, 2004, http://www.misszoot.com/2004/08/honor_roll.php.

127. "Reward Our Students with Healthy Foods," *Bowling Green Daily News*, September 5, 2004, http://www.bgdailynews.com/articles/stories/public/200409/05/0e78_editorials.html.

128. Elizabeth Pierce, "Cell Calls Create Capitol Calories," *Rapid City Journal*, December 4, 2003, http://www.rapidcityjournal.com/articles/2004/12/04/legislature/2003/news/811news.txt.

129. Sandi Dolbee, "Faith and the Fork: Is It Time for Religion to Examine Its Role in Expanding Waistlines?" *San Diego Union Tribune*, May 20, 2004, http://www.rickross.com/reference/weighdown/weighdown9.html; *The Simpsons*, "King of the Hill."

130. Cline and Ferraro, "Does Religion Increase the Prevalence and Incidence of Obesity in Adulthood?"

131. "Frequently Asked Questions," *Vineyard Church of Ithaca*, http://www.ithacavineyard.org/faq.php.

132. Tim Carlfeldt, "Cowboy Church: Hallelujahs and Howdys," *Walker County Mes-*

senger, September 7, 2005, http://news.mywebpal.com/news_tool_v2.cfm?pnpID=73 0&show=localnews&NewsID=656795.

133. Joe White, "The Fight for Faith," *Focus on the Family Magazine*, September 2005, http://www.family.org/fofmag/pp/a0037619.cfm.

134. Bea Tate, letter, July 1998, *Inside the Way International*, http://www.empire net.com/~messiah7/ltr_tate.htm.

135. Tony Cook, "Doughnut Giveaway 'About Jesus,'" *Cincinnati Post*, December 22, 2004, http://www.cincypost.com/2004/12/22/dough122204.html.

136. Melissa Scott Sinclair, "One Church's Ministry by Broom, Towel and Toilet Brush," *Style Weekly*, July 22, 2005, http://www.styleweekly.com/article.asp?idarticle =10557.

137. Carol Pipes, "With Free Doughnuts You Get the Gospel," *OnMission.com*, September–October 2000, http://www.onmission.com/site/c.cnKHIPNuEoG/b.829855/k.C615/With_Free_Doughnuts_You_Get_the_Gospel.htm.

138. Ray Furr, "Christian Pastor More Likely to Be Overweight," *Biblical Recorder*, September 6, 2002, http://www.biblicalrecorder.org/content/news/2002/9_6_2002/neo60902christian.shtml.

139. Cline and Ferraro, "Does Religion Increase the Prevalence and Incidence of Obesity in Adulthood?" 278.

140. Walter Johnson, "A Cup of Coffee, a Doughnut, the 'Good Ship Network' and You," *Network for Inclusive Vision Newsletter* 11, no. 2 (2002), http://www.inclusivenet.com/newsletter/2002-spring.asp.

141. Chris Winters, "Doughnuts Help Snare Bear—Sightings in King County Increasing Dramatically," *Kingcountyjournal.com*, June 16, 2005, http://www.kingcountyjournal.com/sited/story/html/209799.

142. Richard Smith, "Nothing Sporting about Bating Bears," *York County Coast Star*, September 4, 2003, http://www.seacoastonline.com/2003news/yorkstar/ys9_4_e1.htm.

143. Bruce Murphy, "What Would Teddy Do?" *The Morning News*, November 11, 2004, http://www.themorningnews.org/archives/opinions/what_would_teddy_do.php.

144. Wayne Pacelle, "Bear Down: Maine Voters Can Show the Moral Character Their Officials Lack," *Humane Society*, 2005, http://www.hsus.org/legislation_laws/wayne_pacelle_the_animal_advocate/bear_down_maine_voters_can_show_the_moral_character_their_officials_lack.html.

145. Ted Williams, "Hunters Close Ranks, and Minds," *High Country News*, March 3, 1997, http://www.hcn.org/servlets/hcn.Article?article_id=3088.

146. Murphy, "What Would Teddy Do?"

147. Ibid.

148. Lance Tapley, "Bear Ethics," *Portlandphoenix.com*, August 13, 2004, http://www.portlandphoenix.com/features/top/ts_multi/documents/04054323.asp.

149. Kevin L. Raye, "Rural Maine Couldn't Bear Economic Impact of Question 2,"

MaineToday.com, October 24, 2004, http://www.mainetoday.com/elections/2004/referendum/041025_041024bearvoteno.shtml.

150. "Dazzling Wedding at Red Hook," *Brooklyn Eagle,* June 26, 1869, 2.

151. Bella English, "Dukin' Donuts," *Boston Globe,* June 27, 2003, http://www.azcentral.com/home/takeout/articles/0627donutwar27.html.

152. Juliette Arai, Wendy Shay, and Franklin A. Robinson Jr. "Krispy Kreme Doughnut Corporation Records, ca. 1937–1997," *American History Archives Center,* http://americanhistory.si.edu/archives/d7594.htm.

153. Miss Zoot, "Krispy Kreme Donut Wedding Cake," *Miss Zoot Blog,* post February 9, 2004, http://www.misszoot.com/i_krispy_kreme/.

154. Jane Longshore, "Hole'y Matrimony," *Black and White,* June 20, 2002, http://www.bwcitypaper.com/1pubicindex.lasso?-token.editorialreferral=30377.111115.

155. "Wedding Cake Out of Doughnuts," *J.,* January 28, 2005, http://www.jewishsf.com/content/2-0-/module/displaystory/story_id/24805/format/html/edition_id/486/display.htm.

156. "Krispy Kreme Celebrates 65th Birthday," *Junk Food News.net,* http://www.junkfoodnews.net/krispykreme.htm.

157. Janet K. Keeler, "Deconstructing Doughnuts," *St. Petersburg Times,* October 16, 2002, http://www.sptimes.com/2002/10/16/news_pf/Taste/dish.shtml.

158. Corinna, "Opinion of the Day," *Sharon and Jake's Forum,* August 15, 2003, http://sharonandjake.com/phpBB2/viewtopic.php?p=2822&sid=e7b2f34d5a9850033 1245528a44993ac.

159. "Dawn & Paul in Rockport, TX," *The Knot.com,* http://weddings.theknot.com/odb/themes/realweddings/weddingview.aspx?id=1935.

160. Liz Nakazawa, "Swahili Studies—In a Doughnut Shop?" *Christian Science Monitor,* May 3, 2005, http://www.csmonitor.com/2005/0503/p14s01-legn.html.

161. "Hole-y Matrimony at Dunkin' Donuts Contest," *Dunkin' Donuts,* http://www.iwantmyweddingatdunkindonuts.com/.

162. "Mickey Lolich," *The Baseball Page,* http://www.thebaseballpage.com/players/lolicmi01.php#Full%20Bio.

163. Kate Houston, "The Year Mickey Lolich Won the World Series," *Detroit News,* http://info.detnews.com/history/story/index.cfm?id=12&category=sports.

164. Stephen Rush, "From Baseball to Business—Former Major League Players Who Are Now Entrepreneurs," *Nation's Business,* October 1996, http://www.findarticles.com/p/articles/mi_m1154/is_n10_v84/ai_18732016.

165. Jane Gross, "Fastballs to Doughnuts," October 9, 1984, D29.

166. "Krispy Kreme Entering United Kingdom," *The Business Journal,* November 14, 2002, http://www.bizjournals.com/triad/stories/2002/11/11/daily32.html.

167. E. J. Mundell, "'America's Oldest Teenager' Gets Serious about Diabetes," *HealthDay,* April 21, 2004, http://www.hon.ch/News/HSN/518499.html.

168. *The Simpsons,* "Carrie."

169. *The Simpsons,* "Treehouse of Horror IV."

170. *The Simpsons,* "Lisa's Date with Density."

171. *The Simpsons,* "Girly Edition."

172. *The Simpsons,* "Treehouse of Horror IV."

173. Ibid.

174. *The Simpsons,* "Tide."

175. *The Simpsons,* "Treehouse of Horror IV."

176. *The Simpsons,* "She of Little Faith."

177. *The Simpsons,* "Treehouse of Horror XI."

178. Jefferson Robbins, "2 British Men Come to Land of Bart and Homer as Winners of Promotional Contest," *State Journal-Register,* December 9, 1999, http://www.snpp.com/other/articles/twobritish.html.

179. Anthony Noguera, "Interview with Homer Simpson," *FHM* 87, no. 3 (1997): 126–27.

180. Merissa Marr and Suzanne Vranica, "Burgers Get Star Billing; White Castle's Movie Role Is Risky Product-Placement; Smoking Pot, Craving 'Slyders,'" *Wall Street Journal,* July 28, 2002, B1.

Bibliography

Alcott, Wm. A. *The Young Housekeeper, Or Thoughts on Food and Cookery.* 6th ed. Boston: Waite, Peirce, 1846.

Allen, Ann. *The Housekeeper's Assistant, Composed upon Temperance Principles, with Instructions in the Art of Making Plain and Fancy Cakes, Puddings, Pastry, Confectionary, Ice Creams, Jellies, Blanc Mange, Also for the Cooking of all the Various Kinds of Meats and Vegetables; With a Variety of Useful Information and Receipts Never before Published.* Boston: James Munroe, 1845.

American Dairy Association. *Grins and Gripes of the Grocer.* Rosemont, Ill.: American Dairy Association, 1953.

Aunt Babette. *"Aunt Babette's" Cook Book: Foreign and Domestic Receipts for the Household: A Valuable Collection of Receipts and Hits for the Housewife, Many of Which Are Not to Be Found Elsewhere.* Cincinnati: Block Publishing and Print Company, 1889.

Bergman, Signe. *Ellis Island Oral History Project, Series KECK, no. 095: Interview of Signe Bergman by Debby Dane, November 25, 1985.* Alexandria, Va.: Alexander Street Press, 2003.

Bernstein, Eldon, and Fred Carstensen. "Rising to the Occasion: Lender's Bagels and the Frozen Food Revolution, 1927–1985." *Business and Economic History* 25, no. 1 (1996): 165–75.

Brown, Joe E. *"You Said a Mouthful."* New York: Doughnut Corporation of America, 1944.

Buist, Ron. *Tales from Under the Rim: The Marketing of Tim Hortons.* Fredericton, New Brunswick: Goose Lane, 2003.

Carter, Sussanah. *The Frugal Housewife, or, Complete Woman Cook; Wherein the Art of Dressing All Sorts of Viands Is Explained in Upwards of Five Hundred Approved Receipts, in Gravies, Sauces, Roasting [etc.] . . . Also the Making of English Wines.*

To Which Is Added an Appendix, Containing Several New Receipts Adapted to the American Mode of Cooking. New York: G. & R. Waite, 1803.

Chapman, G., and Maclean, H. "'Junk Food' and 'Healthy Food': Meanings of Food in Adolescent Women's Culture." *Journal of Nutrition Education* 25, no. 3 (1993): 108–13.

Child, Lydia Maria Francis. *The Frugal Housewife, Dedicated to Those Who Are Not Ashamed of Economy.* 2nd ed. Boston: Carter and Hendee, 1830.

Cline, Krista M. C., and Kenneth F. Ferraro. "Does Religion Increase the Prevalence and Incidence of Obesity in Adulthood?" *Journal for the Scientific Study of Religion* 45, no. 2 (2006): 269–81.

The Cook Not Mad, Or Rational Cookery; Being a Collection of Original and Selected Receipts, Embracing Not Only the Art of Curing Various Kinds of Meats and Vegetables for Future Use, but of Cooking in Its General Acceptance, to the Taste, Habits, and Degrees of Luxury, Prevalent with the American Publick, in Town and Country. To Which Are Added, Directions for Preparing Comforts for the SICKROOM; Together with Sundry Miscellaneous Kinds of Information, of Importance to Housekeepers in General, Nearly All Tested by Experience. Watertown, Mass: Knowlton & Rice, 1831.

Corson, Juliet. *Miss Corson's Practical American Cookery and Household Management.* New York: Dodd, Mead, 1886.

Criddle, JoAn D. *Bamboo and Butterflies: From Refugee to Citizen.* Auke Bay: East/West Bridge Publishing House, 1992.

Crum, J. Howard. *Beauty and Health: A Course in Loveliness.* Cleveland: World Publishing, 1941.

Davis, Charles. *Cambodian Doughnut Dreams.* Boulder: Throughline Productions, 1990. Short film.

De Tocqueville, Alexis. *Democracy in America.* New York: Scrathcherd and Adams, 1839.

Dunn, Mary. *Ellis Island Oral History Project, Series KECK, no. 127: Interview of Mary Dunn by Dana Gumb, January 23, 1986.* Alexandria, Va.: Alexander Street Press, 2003.

Fox, Minnie C. *The Blue Grass Cook Book.* New York, Fox, Duffield, 1904.

Fullstandigaste Svensk-Americakansk Kokbok/Swedish-English Cookbook. Chicago: Engberg-Holmberg, 1897.

Gabaccia, Donna R. *We Are What We Eat: Ethnic Food and the Making of Americans.* Cambridge: Harvard University Press, 1998.

Glasse, Mrs. [Hannah]. *The Art of Cookery Made Plain and Easy.* Alexandria, Virginia: Cottom and Stewart, 1805.

Goldsmith, Marsha F. "Walking in Beauty at Sage Memorial Hospital," *Journal of the American Medical Association* 288 (July 2003): 29–30.

Hearn, Lafcadio. *La Cuisine Creole: A Collection of Culinary Recipes, from Leading Chefs and Noted Creole Housewives, Who Have Made New Orleans Famous for Its Cuisine.* New Orleans: F. F. Hansell & Bro., 1885.

Hess, John L., and Karen Hess. *The Taste of America*. Urbana: University of Illinois Press, 2000.

Horowitz, Daniel. *The Morality of Spending: Consumers, Household Budget Experts, and Social Critics in the United States, 1895–1940*. Baltimore: Johns Hopkins University Press, 1985.

Howland, Mrs. E. A. *The American Economical Housekeeper and Family Receipt Book*. Cincinnati: H. W. Derby, 1845.

Hurley, Andrew. *Diners, Bowling Alleys, and Trailer Parks: Chasing the American Dream in Postwar Consumer Culture*. New York: Basic Books, 2001.

Irving, Washington. *A History of New York, from the Beginning of the World to the End of the Dutch Dynasty. Containing Among many Surprising and Curious Matters, the Unutterable Ponderings of Walter the Doubter, the Disastrous Projects of William the Testy, and the Chivalric Achievements of Peter the Headstrong, the Three Dutch Governors of New Amsterdam; Being the Only Authentic History of the Times That Ever Hath Been, or Ever Will Be Published*. New York: Inskeep & Bradsford, 1809.

Jackson, Kenneth T. *Crabgrass Frontier: The Suburbanization of the United States*. New York: Oxford University Press, 1985.

Jakle, John A., and Keith A. Sculle. *Fast Food: Roadside Restaurants in the Automobile Age*. Baltimore: Johns Hopkins University Press, 1999.

Jasinski, Josephine. *Ellis Island Oral History Project, Series KECK, no. 128: Interview of Josephine Jasinski by Dana Gumb, January 23, 1986*. Alexandria, Va.: Alexander Street Press, 2003.

Jones, Evan. *American Food: The Gastronomic Story*. 2nd ed. New York: Random House, 1981.

Kazanjian, Kirk, and Amy Joyner. *Making Dough: The 12 Secret Ingredients of Krispy Kreme's Success*. Hoboken, N.J.: Wiley, 2004.

Kear, Andrew. "If You've Seen One You've Seen Them All? Architectural Space, Tim Horton's, and the Uncertainty of Context." *Journal for the Arts, Sciences and Technology* 2, no. 2 (2004): 81–85.

King, Elizabeth. *How to Run a Successful Party*. New York: Doughnut Corporation of America, 1945.

Klein, Naomi. *No Logo: Money, Marketing, and the Growing Anti-Corporate Movement*. New York: Picador USA, 1999.

Lang, Lucy Fox Robins. *Tomorrow Is Beautiful*. New York: Macmillan, 1948.

Leslie, Miss [Eliza]. *Directions for Cookery, In Its Various Branches*. 10th ed. Philadelphia: E. L. Carey & A. Hart, 1840.

———. *Seventy-five Receipts for Pastry, Cakes, and Sweetmeats*. 4th ed. Boston: Munroe and Francis, 1832.

Levenstein, Harvey. *Paradox of Plenty: A Social History of Eating in Modern America*. Berkeley: University of California Press, 2003.

Levy, E., P. Levy, C. Le Pen, and A. Basdevant. "The Economic Cost of Obesity: The

French Situation." *International Journal of Obesity Related Metabolic Disorders* 19, no. 11 (1995): 788–92.

Lincoln, Mrs. A. D. *Mrs. Lincoln's Boston Cook Book: What to Do and What Not to Do in Cooking.* Boston: Roberts Brothers, 1884.

Melville, Herman. *Moby Dick.* 1851. Oxford: Oxford University Press, 1999.

Mintz, Sidney W. *Tasting Food, Tasting Freedom: Excursions into Eating, Culture, and the Past.* Boston: Beacon Press, 1996.

Murphy, Kevin D. "A History of the Doughnut," *Food History News* 15, no. 1 (2003): 1+.

Penfold, Steve. "'Eddie Shack Was No Tim Horton': Donuts and the Folklore of Mass Culture in Canada." In *Food Nations: Selling Taste in Consumer Societies*, ed. Warren Belasco and Philip Scranton, 48–66. New York: Routledge, 2002.

———. *The Social Life of Donuts: Commodity and Community in Postwar Canada.* Ph.D. dissertation submitted to faculty of Graduate Studies, York University, 2002.

Randolph, Mrs. Mary. *The Virginia Housewife: Or, Methodical Cook.* Baltimore: Plaskitt & Cugle, 1838.

Ritzer, George. *The McDonaldization of Society.* Thousand Oaks, Calif.: Pine Forge Press, 1996.

Rose, Peter G. *The Sensible Cook: Dutch Foodways in the Old and the New World.* Syracuse, N.Y.: Syracuse University Press, 1998.

Rosenberg, William, and Jessica Brilliant Keener. *Time to Make the Donuts: The Founder of Dunkin' Donuts Shares an American Journey.* New York: Lebhar-Friedman Books, 2001.

Smith, Seba. *My Thirty Years Out of the Senate. By Major Jack Downing.* New York: Oaksmith, 1859.

Sorensen, Christine. *Ellis Island Oral History Project, Series DP, no. 058: Interview of Christine Sorensen by Nancy Dallet, November 16, 1989.* Alexandria, Va.: Alexander Street Press, 2004.

Steinberg, Sally Levitt. *The Donut Book: The Whole Story in Words, Pictures, and Outrageous Tales.* North Adams, Mass.: Storey Publishing, 2004.

Stewart, Elinore Pruitt. *Letters of a Woman Homesteader.* New York: Houghton-Mifflin, 1914.

Stowe, Harriet Beecher. *Pogunac People: Their Loves and Lives.* Hartford: Stowe-Day Foundation, 1977.

Susman, Warren I. *Culture as History: The Transformation of American Society in the Twentieth Century.* New York: Parthenon Books, 1984.

Thoreau, Henry David. *Cape Cod.* Boston: Houghton-Mifflin, 1906.

———. *Walden; or, Life in the Woods.* Boston: Ticknor and Fields, 1854.

Trager, James. *The Food Chronology: A Food Lover's Compendium of Events and Anecdotes, From Prehistory to the Present.* New York: Henry Holt, 1995.

Veblen, Thorstein. *The Theory of the Leisure Class: An Economic Study of Institutions.* New York: MacMillan, 1902.

Wilcox, Estelle Woods. *Buckeye Cookery, and Practical Housekeeping: Compiled from Original Recipes.* Minneapolis: Buckeye, 1877.

Woods, Bertha M. *Foods of the Foreign-Born in Relation to Health.* Boston, Whitcomb & Barrows, 1922.

Index

Paul R. Mullins is associate professor of anthropology at Indiana University–Purdue University, Indianapolis. In 2000 he received the John L. Cotter Award in Historical Archaeology for his first book, Race and Affluence: An Archaeology of African American and Consumer Culture (1999).